Farewell With Grace ~ For Loved Ones

Testimonial

Farewell with Grace represents one of the most influential 'training manuals' I have read. Training manual? For what? For the inevitable reality facing all of us: death. Our own death, for sure, but the deaths of our loved ones, too. Thankfully, most people live semi-privileged lives, relatively free from intense mental and physical trauma. My 20+ years in the field of chronic pain research and the connections of the mind and body shows the average person is not adequately prepared for the spectrum of experiences life presents. So when trauma happens people are at the 'whim of the gods' and most often swing towards post-traumatic stress disorder (PTSD). With proper training, however, mental and physical resiliency can become strong, leading to a state known as post-traumatic growth order (PTGO).

Farewell with Grace combines intense personal experience, profound insight, cutting-edge understanding, practical and legal tips and humour to help anyone from any walk of life to prepare for the inevitable and ultimate life event. After reading it, I can say I am much better prepared to enter PTGO and help others attain the same glorious state during the dying experience. A life well lived is extended and maximised by a death well shared – this book provides the wisdom to walk that path.

Gary Keil, PhD, RPh
Strategic Holistic Healthcare Expert
PhD in NeuroPharmacology

Dedication

For those who love,
For those who care,
For those who share the end journey of a loved one in this physical realm.

May you find some comfort, support and guidance in the following pages.

Acknowledgements

A life of service requires that one not only gives, but also receives so that one can continue to serve. I have been blessed with so many people who give that I am truly enabled to serve.

First and foremost, as always, is my beloved hubby Reid. Your patience, your faith, your support, your belief, your love, your being my safe space when I need to recharge . . . every fibre of your being tells every fibre of my being how important we are to each other. Thank you, my darling, for always being there for me and with me. I adore you.

For my clients – both the dying and their loved ones – thank you for all that you have taught me as well. I have been honoured to serve you and humbled in your presence at the blessing it was to share in your experience.

To all the fabulous cheer squad who have supported me from the sidelines – there are too many of you to mention, but please know how deeply your support is felt and appreciated.

To the wonderful friends who cast their gaze over this book in its various stages, thank you so much for your valued input and feedback. It truly is about making this book as powerful and beneficial as it can be.

To my brilliant editor Alex and her team – you've done it again. Thanks for your gifts.

And last, but never least, to my loved ones who have gone before and who, through their experiences and journeys, started me on this road. Thank you for all that you have taught me and for continuing to be with me and mess with my mind from your side of the realm.

FAREWELL WITH GRACE
FOR LOVED ONES

Support for you as you support your dying loved one

www.SpiritualPalliativeCare.com

The information provide in this book is general in nature and not specific advice. Please seek assistance for individual support for your particular situation and circumstances.

Soft Cover ISBN : 978-0-9874198-4-2
EBook ISBN : 978-0-9874198-5-9

For feedback and public speaking requests, please contact Sharon at Peace@SpiritualPalliativeCare.com

Cover design by Reid Tregoning
www.Sharreid.digital

Author's photo Karen Cougan
Above See Level Photography
www.karencougan.com

Editing by Alex Mitchell – Author Support Services
www.AuthorSupportServices.com

About the author

With a background including banking, telecommunications, customer service and administrative management, along with having been an executive PA and owning/running a 4½ star luxury couples' retreat, Sharon Tregoning certainly has not come to her current work in a 'normal' way. Answering a soul calling and with an absolute belief that the dying and death experience can be improved for the betterment of all concerned – the dying, their loved ones and the medical professionals – Sharon founded Spiritual Palliative Care.

Part of her mission is to bring dying and death out of the closet, so that they are again just an accepted part of our life cycle and not something to cause paralysing fear. It's also about helping people know that they can make their end-of-life experiences powerful, meaningful and, most of all, personal.

Sharon is a facilitator of healing, a psychic/medium, a spiritual counsellor, a published author, an inspiring public speaker and a holder of a Bachelor of Divinity (working on her Masters) and a Diploma in Counselling. She is the Vice President for Dying With Dignity Queensland. One question guides all her work with the dying: "What will give you peace?"

Spiritual Palliative Care
www.SpiritualPalliativeCare.com

Spiritual Counselling
www.SharonTregoning.com

Preface

Sharing the end journey with a loved one who is dying is a heartbreaking and soul-shattering experience. You sit and watch as this person you have known and loved gradually fades. You see their vibrancy, their life force, gradually extinguish. And of course you have anticipatory grief, knowing that their physical life is going to cease before you want it to.

The flipside of all of this is that you have the gift of knowing. And it is a gift that not everyone gets. Because you have the awareness that your loved one is dying, healing can be undertaken, loving words said, loving actions carried out, issues resolved, precious memories created. It's a very different place, compared to everyday normality, energetically speaking, in which to exist.

I have experienced the deaths of quite a number of my relatives in a palliative context. The most intimate of those were my Dad, my only sister Bess (aka Liz to the rest of the world) and my Mum. I know how bloody heartbreaking watching someone die who is precious to you can be. But I also know that there will be many precious gifts you will receive through the experience, if you allow yourself to see them.

While it can be a spirit crushing experience, if we allow our dying loved ones to have a good death as defined by them, and if we work towards self-awareness, honouring the experience and our needs, then we can reduce, if not eliminate, regret from our grieving experience. Regret just complicates grief. We can't do anything about the coming lack of the physical presence of our loved one, but we can work on the regret aspect.

Through my business, Spiritual Palliative Care, I have worked with a number of loved ones of the dying who really struggle with needing some support, knowing what to expect and knowing how to be. This is to be expected, as we as a community don't get any training in how to share that journey with a dying loved one, and it's not something we are exposed to as much as in days gone by.

My hope is to change that. To give you the support and guidance you need to make sharing this journey a bit easier, to share the load with you, to educate you around what you and/or your dying loved one may experience, to reduce the aspect of regret from your grieving experience and, finally, to help your dying loved one to know a good dying and death experience, as defined by them.

All of this is designed to help you say farewell to your dying loved one with grace and peace.

Contents

Introduction

The purpose for this book is truly very simple – as the best ideas often are. The aim is two-fold:

- To support you with practical ideas, tools, tips and strategies as you share the dying and death experience of a loved one
- To eliminate or reduce the presence of regret in your grieving experience

In my experiences with my own precious loved ones who have undergone a palliative journey, my connection to the Divine, study, reading and more study, and my work with my palliative clients, I have gained a lot of knowledge about what makes a difference – what helps and what doesn't. In a society and culture where talking about dying and death is not commonplace or encouraged, I feel it is important to share this information to help you.

We are not schooled in anything related to the dying and death experience, and we have become very skilled at isolating our dying friends and family from our worlds and insulating ourselves from the experience – both from their perspective and ours. Long gone are the days when dying and death were commonplace in our communities, giving us understanding and some idea of what to expect. And of course, what we don't know or understand, we fear.

This book aims to counter that. One of my grand aims (or big, hairy, audacious goals) is for dying and death to once again be accepted parts of our natural life cycle as human beings. For we will all die.

Above all else, my aim for this book is that it be a practical tool to help you, a resource that you will return to time and again as you need some support. Certainly you can read it from cover to cover, or you may feel more inclined to scan the contents and say to yourself, "Ooooooh, that's what I need some help with." There are no rules here – you have enough going on in your life without me throwing rules on how to use this book at you!

This book aims to serve you, to support you, to uplift you and to wrap you in a virtual warm hug when you need it the most. To know that there is somewhere who has walked a similar path, who has an understanding of what you are feeling and wants to guide you along the way. To hold your hand and say "You can do this" through the crappy times (and they will be there) and "That's to be treasured" when you see some of the beautiful gifts that can arrive through the journey (and there will be some of these too).

Throughout the book you will notice I use the term 'loved ones.' For me, this is an all-encompassing term for the special and treasured people in our lives. They are not necessarily relatives – after all, we all know some horror stories about relatives who are definitely not loved ones. The term does, of course, include those incredibly special soul families that we create for ourselves – the friends who totally get us, understand us and accept us just as we are.

This book is also a memoir of my experiences with my loved ones – the good, the bad, the great and the downright ugly. Because I believe there is much value in sharing stories and experiences.

So make a cuppa, make yourself comfy and let's start working together to support you on this journey with your loved one.

Chapter 1. Dying and Death – Where We Are Today and How We Got Here

Dying and death within our communities has changed substantially in the last century or so. Not only the where and how, but also the ages at which we die. The following statistics are according to the Grattan Institute report *Dying Well,* which was released in September 2014:

- In 1900, 25% of the population died before the age of five – mostly from infectious diseases – and only 5% died after the age of 85
- In 2011, less than 1% of the population died before age five and more than 40% died after the age of 85, largely from chronic illnesses

In years gone by, people would die at home, in their communities and surrounded by their loved ones. Death would often be quick and not the drawn-out experience that we often know these days.

For the most part, we knew how to be with our dying and knew what to expect. It was an experience with which we were acquainted as it was commonplace.

After World War II, we saw the increase of hospitals and improvements in sanitation and medical treatment. Dying moved from being in the community to occurring in hospitals. According to Dr. JoQuim Madrenas, professor of Microbiology, Immunology and Medicine at the University of Western Ontario, dying stopped being a part of life.
A century ago, death was a public event with the deathbed acting as one of the central features of community life. "People basically saw a death as a social gathering in which the person dying was supported by the community, and the community basically got some type of closure from the dying person," says Madrenas.

http://www.cbc.ca/news/health/a-brief-history-of-death-and-dying-1.1115800

The move into hospitals and hospital-based care, while it has offered us many improvements, has also had another perhaps unintended consequence in that the patient can get lost in the system. They become a patient, associated exclusively with their illness or disease, not a whole and many-faceted person. The focus becomes more about treatment and potential cure, rather than about quality of life and care goals.

BJ Miller, Executive Director of Zen Hospice in San Francisco, summarised this perfectly in a TED talk he gave in March 2015.

"Healthcare was designed with diseases, not people, at its centre. Which is to say, of course, it was badly designed. And nowhere are the effects of bad design more heartbreaking or the opportunity for good design more compelling than at the end of life, where things are so distilled and concentrated. There are no do-overs."

The modern hospice movement was founded by Dame Cicely Saunders when the world's first purpose-built hospice was opened in 1967. It combined teaching, clinical research, expert pain and symptom relief, and holistic care to meet the physical, social, psychological and spiritual needs of its patients, as well as those of their families and friends. The founder introduced the concept of total pain management, which included physical, emotional, social and spiritual distress.

There are two quotes from Dame Cicely Saunders that I particularly love:

"You matter because you are you, and you matter to the end of your life. We will do all we can, not only to help you die peacefully, but also to live until you die."

" How people die remains in the memory of those who live on."

These two quotes are pivotal for me as they perfectly encapsulate the aims of my business and of serving you through this book.

And so we find ourselves today where we have become so skilled at isolating our dying and insulating ourselves from the experience that we do not see it, we do not know it and we don't know what to expect from it. And so we fear it. This causes us to avoid death and dying even more.

The busyness of our lives supports us in avoiding this experience as well – little knowing that in the long term this can actually cause more problems for us. The other reason that we are not exposed to dying and death as much is that people are dying much older. I had one friend in her early 40s who had not ever experienced the death of a loved one.

Part of my mission is to bring dying and death back out of the closet into which we as a community have placed them. To allow them to be seen, once again, as natural parts of the human life cycle – for we are all going to die. Armed with that fact, the journey for me becomes about making it as peaceful and positive an experience as possible – for both the person dying and their loved ones.

Chapter 2. Required Paperwork and Documentation

If you are the person who does or will have the responsibility for your loved one relating to their health, treatment and/or estate after they die, you need to ensure that all of this is properly and legally documented. While in the end the responsibility for creating and completing the documentation rests with your loved one, having all the paperwork in place ensures that their wishes are formally documented and that you are legally enabled and protected in carrying them out.

The information provided in this section is general in nature and not specific to the needs of you or your loved one. It also relates to my home state of Queensland, Australia. Please consult a legal practitioner appropriate to the geographical region where your loved one lives to ensure that you meet all local requirements.

The documents I will cover are wills, enduring powers of attorney and advance health directives. This paperwork is also important for you to have, so I have written most of this section from the perspective of you preparing it for yourself.

Wills

We often think of wills as being only for those with a lot of assets. And while that is true, we can forget about hidden assets – specifically, I'm thinking of superannuation.

When I was 20, I think my total assets would have been less than $2,000, and that included my car! We didn't have superannuation, which most often these days includes a life insurance component. So it is imperative that any person over the age of 18 has a valid and current will.

If you die without a valid and current will, your estate will then be handed to the State Trustees in your state (if you live in Australia), who will then determine who gets what. Here are a couple of examples, taken from the State Trustees Queensland website, of what can happen if you don't have a valid and current will:

- *James was born in New Zealand and immigrated to Australia, where he moved to a Queensland mining town.*

  James lived in a de facto relationship with his partner, Karen, for over 20 years and helped raise Karen's children from a previous relationship. These children lived with him until they were adults.

Sadly, Karen died before James, and in her will she left him her estate. James continued the close relationship he shared with Karen's children for many years.

When James died without a will, Karen's now adult children did not receive any of his estate, including the family home where they had lived their entire lives. James's estate was given to a brother living in New Zealand.

If only James had made a will outlining who he wanted to receive his estate, things would have turned out differently.

- *Kylie was 22 years of age when she died in a tragic accident. Kylie did not have a will, and her estate received a $2M insurance payout due to her accidental death.*

  Because she had not made a will, Kylie's estate was divided with 50% allocated to each of her parents. This happened even though Kylie's father deserted the family when Kylie was six months old and did not pay a cent of child support.

  The family claims there is no way Kylie would have wanted her dad to receive anything.

If only Kylie had made her wishes known!

Having a valid and current will is the *only* way to guarantee that your estate will be allocated in the way you wish. And it doesn't need to be an expensive exercise. Will kits can be purchased for less than $50, but clearly it is appropriate to suggest that you seek legal advice as to what is right for you in your particular situation.

A few other things must be taken into consideration, depending on your particular circumstances.

- If you are a single parent with kids under the age of 18, you will need to include arrangements for them in terms of a guardian.
- If you have any pets (as with underage kids), determine what arrangements you wish to occur for your beloved furry (or non-furry) friend(s).
- If you have any particularly precious or treasured mementos, especially jewellery, that you wish to go to someone specific, ensure that this is documented.

Covering things of this nature now will save a lot of grief and heartache later for those left behind.

The other aspect to consider when making your will is who you will list as your executor(s). They will do the liaising with all the relevant organisations with whom you have a relationship (think banks, utilities, clubs, service organisations, etc.) to not only advise them of your passing and finalise accounts, but to organise the sale of any assets and finally to ensure that your estate is allocated as you have expressed in your will.

This is not necessarily an easy or straightforward task. While some people think it is an honour to ask someone to fulfil this role (and it is), you must also consider whether that person is equipped and able to carry out the role, particularly if you have a complex estate. You may want to consider having joint executors or even engaging a legal firm or utilising the State Trustees to handle this on your behalf. Be aware though, that if you utilise either a legal firm or the State Trustees, you will incur extra costs for your estate.

As your loved one knows they are on their end journey, see if they can think about consolidating bank accounts and cancelling memberships, store cards, and other accounts they know they will not need. While this can be a little confronting, it will make the task of finalising their estate infinitely easier for their executor(s). Another suggestion is to have everything listed in a spreadsheet or other document – bank accounts, utilities, store cards, memberships, medical professionals and anyone else that will need to be notified of their passing.

These days, consideration also must be given to social media accounts. Facebook, for example, has a legacy policy whereby someone can be nominated to have some limited functionality on behalf of another person, including being able to post after their death.

Enduring Power of Attorney

An enduring power of attorney is a document that will give whoever you nominate the ability to control all of your affairs – financial, medical, personal, etc. It only comes into force and effect when you have lost the mental capacity to make decisions on your own behalf.

The guidelines for enduring powers of attorney do vary between each state and territory here in Australia, so it is important that you understand the requirements relevant to where you live.

An enduring power of attorney can only be created while you have the mental capacity to complete and authorise it, so it is important to have a current document.

Having a current enduring power of attorney is important, even if you are not ill and/or dying. Think if something unexpected were to happen, such as a car accident. What will happen to your financial and health matters if this document is not in place?

Carefully consider who you will appoint as your attorney. You will need to be able to trust this person implicitly, as they will be able to handle all of your financial matters and will also be the one responsible for ensuring that your wishes are carried out in relation to medical preferences for treatment and other things.

Your attorney does not need to be the same person you appoint as executor of your will. (As with your executor(s), you may also designate more than one individual with the power of attorney.) However, the enduring power of attorney document ceases to have power when you die and the responsibility for managing your affairs then transfers to the executor(s) of your estate.

When you have completed your document and had it properly witnessed, make sure that it is kept in a safe place along with your other legal documents. Ensure that your attorney(s) will know where to find it when the time comes.

Advance Health Directives

Like enduring powers of attorney, the regulations and guidelines around advance health directives vary from state to state, so check with the relevant authorities in your state/territory as to what you need to do.

An advance health directive stipulates what you do and don't want to happen. This is particularly important if you have specific requirements, such as stipulating a 'Do Not Resuscitate' order under certain circumstances. The advance health directive only comes into force and effect when you are no longer able to communicate your wishes and/or you no longer have full mental capacity.

It is recommended that when completing this document, you do so with the guidance of your medical professional. In some places (such as here in Queensland), your doctor must also authorise it before it can be witnessed.

You don't need to be ill or dying to complete one of these documents. You can use it to capture your wishes at any stage in life, provided you are over 18 years of age.

An advance health directive will cover any specific religious beliefs that will have an impact on your treatment – e.g., no blood transfusions or blood products. It can cover who is *not* to be contacted about your treatment and also what life-preserving techniques you do and don't approve.

If you are in favour of euthanasia, you cannot stipulate that you wish to be euthanised as this is against current law. You can, however, state, "I request that I be given sufficient medication to control my pain, even if this hastens my death."

All of this paperwork may seem cumbersome and tedious, but it is vitally important in both capturing the wishes of your loved one and also making sure that the necessary legal permissions are in place if you need to act on their behalf.

Chapter 3. What Your Loved One Is Experiencing

Up until your loved one was advised that their time in this life was coming to an end, they may not have thought that one day they would die. Many people don't, and it's certainly not a commonplace topic for conversation in our society today.

When they were advised that their lifespan was now limited, they may have had one of the following responses:

- Absolute fear of dying
- Relief at what they have instinctively known if they have had a prolonged illness
- Total shock at the diagnosis
- Resentment or anger
- Numbness and disbelief
- Any number of other possibilities

There is actually no 'normal' response – only what is right for them and where they are in their life journey.

It's worth reviewing the work of Dr Elisabeth Kübler-Ross at this stage. She did extensive work with people on their end journeys, creating a model which includes the stages that people experience. I have included quotes relevant to each of the five stages from her book *On Death and Dying*:

- ***Denial*** – *"Since in our unconscious mind we are all immortal, it is almost inconceivable that we too have to face death." "Denial functions as a buffer after unexpected shocking news, allows the patient to collect himself and, with time, mobilise other, less radical defences."*

- ***Anger*** – *"The problem here is that few people place themselves in the patient's position and wonder where this anger might come from. Maybe we too would be angry if all our life activities were interrupted prematurely."*

- ***Bargaining*** – *"The terminally ill patient . . . knows, from past experiences, that there is a slim chance that he may be rewarded for good behaviour and be granted a wish for special services. His wish is most always an extension of life, followed by the wish for a few days without pain or physical discomfort."*

- ***Depression*** – *"When the terminally ill patient can no longer deny his illness . . . his numbness or stoicism, his anger and rage will soon be replaced with a great sense of loss. This loss may have many facets. What we often tend to forget, however, is the preparatory grief that the terminally ill patient has to undergo in order to prepare himself for his final separation from this world."*

- ***Acceptance*** – *"He will have been able to express his previous feelings, his envy for the living and the healthy, his anger at those who do not have to face their end so soon. He will have mourned the impending loss of so many meaningful people and places and he will contemplate his coming end with a certain degree of quiet expectation."*

You may find that your loved one experiences some or all of these, that they miss some completely, that they experience some at the same time or that they experience them in a completely different order. Again, there is no normal, just what is right for their journey.

My Mum went pretty much straight into acceptance, but there were periods of denial and anger that came into her experience in the last few weeks – more on that later.

The important aspect for your loved one is that they feel and believe that they are either working towards or have achieved acceptance.

Accepting that they are on their end journey does not mean that they won't have days where they wish things were different. They may have days when it is all so very overwhelming. It can be very confronting for them to know that they are reaching their life's end, and there may be times when they genuinely do not want this to be happening. This is an ongoing journey, and hopefully they will attain an overall sense of acceptance.

Once they have achieved this acceptance, the rest of their journey can become so much easier. They may find the following changes as a result:

- Things don't seem quite so overwhelming
- Plans become easier to make
- They may find themselves having precious and treasured conversations with those closest to them
- They may find they sleep better
- They may find that some pain decreases
- They may find an increase in energy
- They will certainly find emotional relief, like a weight has been lifted from their shoulders

I firmly believe that if we can address most, if not all, of the dying person's spiritual and emotional challenges, their physical pain and other symptoms will be reduced. (Of course, proving that theory is a whole other conversation!)

One thing that may result for your loved one is a deep and soulful questioning of all that they have previously believed to be true. This can even take the form of an existential crisis. Being confronted with your own mortality can be quite shocking for some people, particularly if they don't already have a deep sense of peace in their lives.

You may discover the same reaction within yourself. When you see precious loved ones die and have that experience thrust firmly in your face, it truly gives you a very different perspective on the world, if you choose to allow it to do so. Things that once seemed so important now seem quite trivial. Activities, friendships, work roles, relationships – all take on a very different focus.

Understand that no matter how informed your loved one is about what to expect as their journey unfolds, and no matter how many other end journeys they may have witnessed, there will still be new experiences for them. Sometimes these can be scary. Give your loved one some time, space and understanding when 'stuff' happens. And give yourself the same gift.

Chapter 4. Being Self-Aware and Authentic

Being Self-Aware

It is simply not possible for me to overestimate just how important this is – and not even just in the experience that you are sharing with your loved one, but in the rest of your life as well. Self-awareness is actually the most powerful gift that you can give yourself.

Being aware of self is to be living consciously and making informed choices in all that you think, feel and do. It means taking the time to think through things, being aware of your feelings, and knowing what you do, when you do it and why. Being conscious means being fully present in the moment, whether it feels it good, bad or neutral. These are just meanings that we allocate to experiences – in truth they all just 'are'.

I've had many of what I called 'bad' experiences at first which, with the benefit of hindsight, time, and sometimes patience and love, have actually turned out to be some of the best experiences of my life given what I have learned from them.

In my belief, most of our society exists in an unconscious state. Just look at all of the news media, TV shows, movies and social media. All of it is designed to program us to behave in certain ways, to look certain ways, to buy certain things, and so on. And it actively encourages us to judge ourselves and each other on our choices.

I truly don't believe that most people make conscious choices about their work, how they spend their time, and how they treat themselves and others. I believe that they are coming from a place of expectation by others, and that sometimes it is easier to just go with the flow. What people miss in the process of this is the fullness of life the opportunity to live their lives with peace and contentment, even when faced with challenges. I believe that people who do not live in a conscious state are depriving themselves of life's greatest and often most simple blessings – the love of true friends, the peace that comes with acceptance of who we are as individuals, the gifts we bring to this life and the beauty in nature.

I implore you to choose to live in full consciousness. Life becomes a lot more colourful when you do. Consciousness is also the birthplace of change. You already have the capacity to change, but that change usually does not come from a place of understanding or purpose. You may simply be changing for the sake of it or because it's what you believe is right for you . . . but this is often superficial change.

You see this a lot in fashion – people start wearing the new season's look without really considering whether it's the right style, shape, colour or pattern for their bodies, personalities and purposes. They are just following the trend of what is being promoted as the 'must wear' this season.

If you are not conscious of how you exist in your life, I would ask you to consider whether you are being truly authentic to yourself, or whether you're just going along with what you believe is easy and expected. Are you operating on automatic pilot, without having any understanding of the drivers behind your thoughts and actions?

In counselling, this is part of what we call 'cognitive behaviour'. It tells us that what we think, how we feel and how we act are all reliant upon our core beliefs and are driven by them. Our thoughts then drive both our emotions and behaviours, which then directly interact with and impact each other.

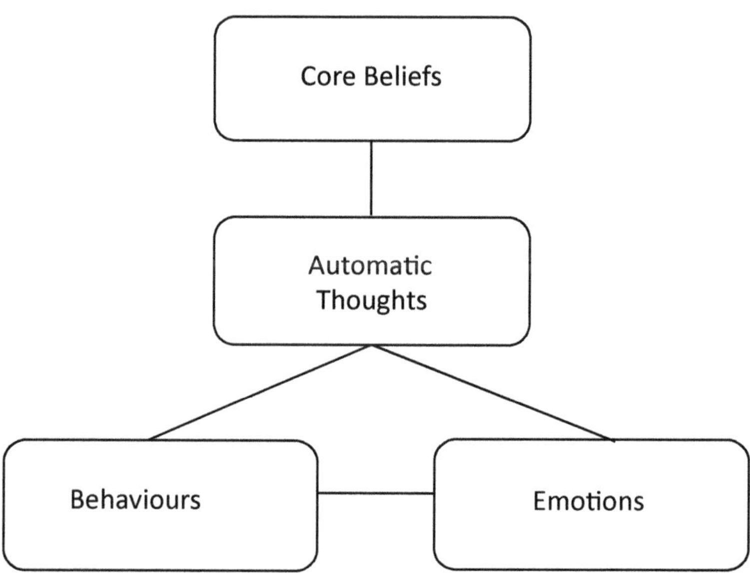

Cognitive Behaviour Therapy is based on the idea that what people think and say about themselves – their attitudes, ideas and ideals – is relevant and important. Let's say a specific external event takes place. Thoughts will occur between that event and our emotional response to it. These thoughts are called 'automatic' and do not come about from deliberation or reasoning. They are also generally involuntary and while we are not normally aware of them, we can be taught to observe them before experiencing the emotional response.

To start changing ourselves, how we feel and how we act, we need to start being aware of what we are thinking and saying, both out loud and to ourselves. And I do need to say here that no change may be needed! I simply urge you to be conscious of your choices and make informed decisions, not just go along with things because that's what you've always done. As the saying goes, "If you always do what you've always done, you'll always get what you've always got". Makes sense, really!

This is all specifically relevant within the context of sharing the end journey with a loved one. Just like they will, you will probably experience a wide variance in your thoughts, behaviours and emotions. Having self-awareness enables you to go a little deeper in your soul-searching to understand what may be really going on for you in terms of how you are responding to their end-of-life journey.

To give you an example of this, my sister Bess (aka Liz to the rest of the world) was advised of a diagnosis of breast cancer in early 2003. My core belief was that breast cancer was a familial thing – remember, we're talking way back in 2003, long before the knowledge and awareness we have today. My first and automatic thought was, "What does this mean for me?" Add into this mix that I had had a breast lump investigated and removed four years prior, so of course that upped the ante for me in terms of expectation. My emotional response, in relation to myself, was one of fear.

My reactions were automatic and instantaneous – no conscious consideration went into my thought process and emotional response. We often see the same thing in relation to people receiving a diagnosis of cancer. No matter what type or what stage, when people hear that someone has cancer, they automatically interpret it as a death sentence. But of course, it's not always true. I really love the phrase "Cancer is a word, not a sentence."

So hit the pause button, do some navel-gazing, spend some time with yourself (it's really not that scary, I promise) and get to know yourself a little better. Get an understanding of what makes you tick, what triggers you have, what feels and doesn't feel comfortable for you in your life. Then perhaps ask yourself the 'why' question with all of these things. Are they your core beliefs or ones that you have accepted and adopted as your own from family, work, social or environmental situations?

Sharing the end journey with a loved one can at times be an incredibly raw emotional experience. Having an awareness and understanding of yourself will make navigating the experience just a little easier.

Authenticity

Along with having self-awareness, being authentic to who you are and what you are experiencing on this journey is pivotal. If you are having a crap day, acknowledge it and allow it to be crap. That doesn't mean it's always going to be crap, but in that moment, at that time, on that day, just be with the crappiness. Someone precious in your world is dying – of course some days are going to be crappy!

The same for good days – this doesn't have to be a full-on, sad, heavy journey 24/7. You are allowed to have a good time, enjoy yourself, smile and, heaven forbid, even laugh. Yes, I know – totally weird concept, huh?

This is about being real to your experience within the context of who you are and how you live your life. I am a sharer (I know, what a massive surprise). Other people in my world are not. It would not be authentic for them to start blurting all over the place what they are experiencing. What am I talking about is being authentic with yourself first and then in ways that are appropriate for how you live in your world.

Being authentic to yourself involves simply noticing and acknowledging what you are experiencing in the moment – that's why we talked about being aware of self before this section. It's about not denying or resisting what you are experiencing, as – trust me – this stuff will come back and bite you on the butt ten-fold and there's a fair chance it will be at the worst possible time.

We are not encouraged to have, let alone acknowledge, 'bad' feelings; these days it's all about making sure that we feel good. The challenge of authenticity lies in learning to acknowledge that we, in our humanness, experience what we call both 'good' and 'bad' feelings. They go with the territory. The truth, though, is that there are no good and bad feelings – they are just feelings. And they are part of our experience, part of who we are. So the process becomes about simply noticing, acknowledging and allowing these feelings to exist.

If you are a sharer, social media is a great facilitator in this respect. No doubt you will have friends in your world who will want to know how things are going. They might not be in your intimate circle, but certainly people who you are comfortable having know what's happening. And in return, this can provide great support for you. I know I took huge comfort from the small comments and messages that people would send to me as I shared about the journey with Mum on Facebook.

Sharing in this way, though, requires a certain level of vulnerability, and that's not something we easily embrace.

> *"Vulnerability is the thing that we embrace as courageous in others, yet shun as a weakness in ourselves."*
>
> –Sharon Tregoning

If you are interested in learning more about vulnerability and authenticity, I highly recommend you check out Brené Brown's work. As of this writing, she has done two TED talks and written a number of books. The first TED talk is called 'The Power of Vulnerability' and the second is 'Listening to Shame'. Essentially, her message is that we cannot selectively numb our emotional experiences – we cannot choose not to experience pain, shame, sadness and other negative feelings, try as we might. We either feel the full spectrum of emotions or we completely shut ourselves down so that we don't feel anything at all.

The great gift of vulnerability is connection to others. It's the sense that even though no other person can truly understand exactly what you are experiencing, you are not alone. There are people who care, there are people who want to support you however they can and there are people to whom you are important; you matter.

Being authentic means being true to yourself in your own world. It's allowing yourself to be truly yourself in all of your human glory – for I believe that is a big part of why we have these human experiences. Yes, I subscribe to the belief that we are spiritual beings having a human experience. We are responsible for and to ourselves for showing up and fully engaging with the circumstances of our lives.

Chapter 5. Making It Special

"Life is not a dress rehearsal."

–Anonymous

Your loved one's dying journey is probably the ultimate 'once in a lifetime' event, unless of course they have already had a near-death experience. For most people, though, this is a one-shot deal. So it is important to do it right – and by right, I mean as defined by your dying loved one. That's the only criteria that really should be in play here. It is *their* dying and death experience, and it needs to be determined by them.

We, who will be left to mourn for our loved ones, have an opportunity if we choose to accept it. I have a theory that there are two aspects to the grieving experience:

- The physical absence of our loved one
- Regret for things said/not said or done/not done, or that our loved one did not have a good death, as defined by them

The physical absence – we can't do anything about that one. Yes, we can connect to our loved ones in spirit directly or through a medium, but it's just not the same as getting to hold them or touch them. My loved ones in spirit show up in my life frequently (and often take great delight in messing with my mind), but I still desperately miss their physical presence.

We can, however, ease the regret aspect of the death of our loved one.

I did a small survey in my business, and over 84% of the respondents indicated that the 'regret' aspect of their grief made the 'physical absence' aspect much worse. And their regrets were mostly based on things *not* said and things *not* done. This is where the opportunity arises for us, as loved ones, to significantly reduce the regret aspect of our grieving experience.

It's about ensuring that our dying loved ones *know* that they are loved. It's about taking steps to heal old wounds, provided that won't cause more pain. It's about making peace with situations that will never be healed. It's about creating precious memories to treasure for years to come. It's about ensuring that life is lived consciously and purposefully. It's about helping your loved one heal experiences that they need to, again providing that this won't cause more pain. It's about ticking things off your loved one's bucket list. It's about doing the little things which truly aren't all that little.

With my Mum, treats become a pretty special part of her end journey. Due to her two lots of hip surgery, she had not been able to drive her car for around six months by the time I arrived to spend her final weeks with her. As she lived on her own, that had meant basically no take-away food. Now, Mum was not a huge take-away person, but she did like to indulge every now and then. I think in the first four nights that I was with her, we worked our way through all her favourites!

Then I discovered a bakery just around the corner from Mum's place that made *the* most divine vanilla slice, and it was so cheap! The custard was creamy smooth and the pastry had just the right amount of flakiness and crunch. This was to become a regular indulgence as it was something that Mum really enjoyed, and I was determined that she get as much pleasure in that final period as possible. I even ended up taking these treats into the hospice once she was there as she really enjoyed them. They also tempted her when not much else did. Managing her diabetes was not a huge issue at this stage. The focus was much more on pleasure, enjoyment and happiness.

This is what I mean by 'the little things not really being little things'. This is your opportunity to create tiny pockets of joy with and for your loved one. Mum and I got gooey and sticky and messy with these vanilla slices and I will treasure those moments forever.

The other thing I will treasure from all of the palliative journeys with my loved ones is the opportunity they provided for deep, honest and soulful conversations. One of the things I love most in my work with my clients is that there is no BS with the dying – they know that is a luxury they just can't afford. The same thing happened with my own loved ones.

You get to share conversations about the stuff that really matters. There were also conversations about the everyday and the seemingly mundane – these were often a blessed distraction from the sometimes heaviness of reality. But the soulful conversations are what I treasure the most. It was such a tremendous blessing to be able to say to them, "I love you so much and I am going to miss you so much. I will be OK and you need to focus on you and what you need, but I will miss you".

The rest of making the dying process special lies in allowing yourself to be guided by your loved one. What do they want? What do they *not* want? This really can be a very special time when precious memories can be created that will last you a lifetime.

Chapter 6. Being PRESENT

Before we learn how to be present with others, we need to learn how to be present with ourselves. We need to be able to have some understanding of what we are experiencing, what we are feeling and what makes us tick if we are to have any hope of being able to connect in this way with others. This ties back again to Chapter 4, Being Self-Aware and Authentic.

Being present with ourselves means being aware of how we respond in various situations and why. It's about understanding our triggers, and about making time and space in our lives to just be with ourselves without any external distraction.

Being present is not something we are encouraged to do in any way these days – instead, we're prompted to fill all of our time with external stimulation, with no time allocated for mindful and even soulful reflection. We're certainly not encouraged to live in a conscious manner where our choices and actions are based on mindful consideration.

Being present in our lives requires us to make time and space to just be with ourselves – to connect deeply with ourselves without any external distraction. Once we have awareness and a genuine desire to live in this way, being present to others, particularly our dying, becomes a whole lot easier.

The word PRESENT is an acronym that provides an easy-to-remember way to help you be PRESENT with your loved one. Let's go through what each letter in the acronym represents.

Present

The first point is, quite literally, to be present. When you are with your loved one, certainly share the everyday and mundane happenings in your life with them – it often gives them a blessed distraction from what may be their reality – however, don't be distracted by these things.

Give your loved one your full attention, because one day soon you will desperately wish that you still could. This is a person who you love and who still has value and worth – treat them this way. If they're not up for talking, maybe read to them, or watch a movie together or just sit in silence with them.

Knowing that your loved one is on their end journey is a gift that not everyone receives – make the most of that time.

Religion/Spirituality

The R stands for Religion/Spirituality. And this one can get a little messy. I encourage you to know, respect and honour the religious/spiritual beliefs of your dying loved one, irrespective of yours. Yep, this is not about you, it's about them.

I heard of one episode involving an atheist man in a hospice. The hospice staff would often tell him they would pray for him, and otherwise talk in ways that were inappropriate in light of this man's beliefs. I have no doubt that these people meant well, but their actions were disrespectful. I don't believe it is ever appropriate to force our beliefs onto others, but it is especially not okay when someone is dying. This journey needs to be about creating a peaceful space as defined by them.

You also often here of people whose religious/spiritual beliefs change markedly after receiving a diagnosis of a terminal illness. This makes sense when they are confronted with their own mortality. What is required of us is to just continue loving this person we have loved, to care for them and to support them in ways that are appropriate for them. That's it.

My sister Bess made a change from being involved with a mainstream Christian church to being part of a Spiritualist one – a very, very different journey for her with a great shift in beliefs.

Enquire

Next up is the first E, which stands for Enquire. Ask about everything and don't assume.

Sometimes our loved one on their end journey may not fully disclose all that they are experiencing as they don't want to cause any 'trouble' or to be a 'bother'. They may not fully express how much pain they are in or what else may be going on for them. This one is particularly important for medical professionals. I have had a number of clients who appreciate how busy and sometimes under-resourced they are, so they have kept some concerns to themselves.

Ask your loved one about their needs – don't assume.

You should also ask about how they want their end journey to be. As mentioned with religious/spiritual beliefs, people's outlooks can often change when they have been diagnosed with a life-limiting illness/ disease. Check in with them, and don't assume that the types of thoughts they have always had are still the same now.

After my sister's journey with cancer and treatment, my Mum said she would never have chemo. That changed after she herself was diagnosed with cancer. She didn't have much, just enough to ensure that she got to meet her first great grandchild.

So the E is for enquire. Don't assume.

Sacred

Next up we have the S, which stands for Sacred.

The dying and death journey is an absolutely sacred experience. Irrespective of what you do and don't believe from a religious/spiritual perspective about what may or may not happen after we physically die, this journey is the end of someone's physical life on this earth. That deserves respect, it deserves reverence, it deserves dignity, it deserves honour and it is sacred.

There are so many ways that this journey can be honoured, and one of those is to ensure that sacred space is created around the person on their end journey. We will cover this in more detail later.

Also ensure that the environment is honoured in terms of the conversations that are held. For you loved ones, this is not the place for disputes or squabbles or even full-on fights. For medical professionals, this is not the place to discuss other patients or workplace experiences. Even if the person dying is unconscious, please ask that everyone in the environment act as if the person can hear all that is said. This is a place for sensitive discussion, laughter, creating more precious memories, and connecting deeply and lovingly.

Encourage

Next, we have the second E, which stands for Encourage.

Encourage the person on their end journey to talk about their experience, as appropriate – the good, the bad, the great and the downright ugly. There will be aspects of all of these on their journey.

Address the elephant in the room – acknowledge the fact that they are actually dying. One of my friends and her family were not made aware that her Mum was dying until a few hours before she actually did, even though she had been in hospital for a couple of weeks. By this stage, her Mum was unresponsive and there was no opportunity for them to do all that they wished to do.

Often there is fear around having discussions of this nature, and the wish not to burden or worry others with the acknowledgment that death is coming – from the perspectives of both the person dying and their loved ones. In actuality, the truth is often freeing. It provides the opportunity to undertake practical matters that need to be addressed. And of course, it allows for things to be said and done that can deliver peace.

I'm not saying this needs to be the only topic of conversation, and certainly don't force anything, but gently and lovingly encourage as appropriate. If there is a strong 'no' coming from the person dying, respect that as they are clearly still struggling with their own journey.

New

Now we look at the N, which stands for New.

There will be new experiences on this journey for you – even if you have experienced the end journey of another loved one and even if you are well-informed as to what to expect. This point is also particularly relevant for medical professionals.

If your dying loved one is a parent, the dynamic between you could completely change and your roles may reverse. For my Mum and I on her end journey, we had to learn how to be in a relationship together that had a completely new dynamic to that which we had had previously. And it took a fair bit of give-and-take on both sides. There were tears for both of us at various times and loving, gentle communication in which we each explained our perspectives. This helped us understand the other's position and work through the challenges that we had.

For my Mum, the greatest issue for her was her loss of independence. Even though at times she knew that some of the choices were sensible in terms of relinquishing things to me, it was still a very great loss that she grieved. This was also part of her journey of accepting that her physical life was coming to an end.

Sharing an end journey needs a whole heap of love, patience and understanding from everyone involved. If you need support and/or you're feeling overwhelmed, please seek assistance.

Treat

Lastly we look at the T, which stands for Treat.

In this context it is about treating the person dying as a whole person, as someone who still has value and worth . . . because they do. They are not just their disease, illness or medical condition – they are not just someone who is dying. This is someone precious in your world.

Just as we wear multiple hats for all the different roles we fulfil in our lives, so too does the person who is dying. They are not just a patient, they are not just someone who is dying, and they are not just a loved one.

I've had people ask me, "How do I talk to someone who is dying?" My answer is always, "How do you talk to someone who is living?" You may need to be sensitive in certain areas, but this person is still alive!

It's truly not difficult to be present with someone on a palliative journey. It simply requires conscious choices from those around them – their loved ones and medical professionals. The gifts that you will receive by being conscious are well worth the effort. And for the person dying, it can make their end journey so much more special.

Chapter 7. Self-Nurturing

Did you just read the title of this chapter and say to yourself, "She's got to be kidding, right"? Or maybe something along the lines of, "I wish"?

Well, guess what? Self-care is imperative . . . unless, of course, martyrdom is in your future or you want to implode.

Do these statements resonate with you?

- You are a giver by nature, not a receiver
- You find it hard to accept any assistance
- You aren't comfortable asking for assistance
- You don't want to complain about how hard it can be at times
- You are exhausted in every possible way – physically, mentally, emotional, spiritually

Because the fabulous caregivers in our world often don't talk about the challenges they may be facing, we have no widespread knowledge about what they may need or want. And often they are so adept at placing the needs of those they care for first that they may not even have conscious awareness of their own needs.

While you will often hear me say that the focus of this journey needs to be on the needs of the person dying, the whole process and experience does need to be managed so that your needs are addressed as well. If they are not taken care of, then you simply won't be able to sustain looking after your loved one. This is irrespective of how much you are doing or involved in the process. The basic fact of the matter is that someone who is precious to you is departing your physical world. Even if you are not geographically present and able to do any practical things, you are still going to be experiencing anticipatory grief; you are still going to be experiencing a vast array of emotions. Those emotions need to be acknowledged and honoured.

All the sayings along the lines of 'not being able to fill the cup of others when yours is empty' are completely spot on. You truly do need to take some responsibility to ensure that your needs are met in terms of eating healthfully and in ways that will sustain you as much as possible, that you take breaks and that you do things just to pamper yourself.

Caring for a loved one on their end journey is incredibly stressful and draining in so many ways. Your focus is completely on them and their needs. However to do this for either a short or sustained period of time, you need to ensure that you look after yourself so that you can continue.

This does not need to be an expensive or even costly exercise. One of the things that really helped me was connecting to nature as I needed – getting my feet in the ocean or onto some grass really helped me to stop and take a breath or 50.

One massive thing that can be done is to allow others to help you out. To emphasise this, I want to share a little story with you. I am a giver by nature. Not much gives me more pleasure than knowing I've helped someone, that I've made a difference and made their day a little brighter, easier or less painful. Doing this absolutely makes my soul sing. And possibly like you, I am not very good at allowing others to do the same for me.

In 2008 I underwent major surgery that had me on an operating table for 11 hours, in hospital for 11 days and then recovering for around three months. It was a huge experience in my life when I *had* to allow others to help me. The insight I received was that I am surrounded by a beautiful lot of people who are also givers by nature – like attracts like. I realized that when I don't allow others to support me, I am denying them the experience of feeling good through being able to help in a practical way. That realisation was huge for me.

Your loved one's dying journey is where you can allow others to do some things to support you. So many people want to help. Allowing them to do so gives you some time for yourself so that you can recharge and then keep going.

Some of the things that people can do to help you are:

- Have them make some food that can go in the freezer
- Get them to help out with some housework or gardening
- Allow them to be with the person you are caring for so that you can go to the hairdresser, see a movie, run errands, or just have a couple of hours to yourself

These are just a few ways that you can get help from others to make the road just a little bit easier for you.

Another crucial element in maintaining your sanity is having a few precious people in your world with whom you can be completely authentic to your experience, knowing they will not judge you and sometimes not even try to fix things for you. These people simply allow you the space to be totally honest in your experience – the good, the bad, the great and the downright ugly. As I said before, all of these will appear on your journey.

On the journey I shared with my Mum, I had a few of these special people – some were pivotal to my experience before Mum died and some afterwards. Along with my hubby Reid, these beautiful soul sisters were precious to me at the time (and still are). Their friendships and the gifts they gave me by providing a little bit of distraction and just being present to me were gifts that I will treasure forever.

One other experience helped me on a particularly bad day. My great-nephew was born two days before I came to stay with Mum. He was actually four weeks premature, and I knew in a heartbeat when I got the call from my nephew to say that their son had been born that he had come early, as Mum wasn't going to make it to his due date. We got Mum to see him within a few days of his birth, and less than two weeks later she was gone.

As I mentioned, I was having a particularly bad day one day – Mum had been angry and I had been the safe space for her to be angry, so it all got directed at me. Emotionally I was really struggling, and it was also the day that I took the power of attorney to be registered on her bank account. It was all getting very real.

I suddenly realised that I was not far from the hospital where my great-nephew was, so I rang my nephew to see if it would be okay to drop in. He said it would, so I did. My nephew and niece were just going to get some lunch, so I got to sit and hold this precious new babe for a while.

What I needed most in that moment was to hold new life. The contrast of my experience was so stark – here I was holding this precious little boy who was less than two weeks old and the rest of the time my focus was entirely on my Mum as her life was drawing to a physical close. I sat there with tears silently streaming down my face.

A couple of the nurses asked if I was okay. I was – it was just the stark contrast that was firmly in my face. I said to my nephew, "You know I just used your son, right?" He said, "Yes". He understood, having lost his own Mum (my sister) five years previously. I was so very deeply thankful in that moment for that new life.

The message I want you to receive loud and clear through this chapter is that you need to acknowledge and honour your own needs so that you can sustain yourself. In most cases this is more likely to be a marathon than a sprint, and it's a highly draining emotional experience that cannot be underestimated. Nurture yourself as you nurture your loved one, and allow others to nurture you as well.

Chapter 8. Big Girl's Panties – Standing Firm as an Advocate

If you are the one who has been charged with the legal responsibilities in relation to the care of your loved one, this is where life can get a bit hairy and sometimes even somewhat unpleasant. But this type of responsibility is one of those necessary yucky things (yes, that is the technical term).

In Chapter 2, we covered some of the legal paperwork that needs to be put in place to ensure that your loved one's wishes are captured and that you are enabled and protected.

That's only one part of the process, though. The other aspect is the actual carrying out of the responsibility and acting on behalf of your loved one. And I am going to assume that if you are reading this book, you are acting out of love for the person who is dying, not just from a place of responsibility.

With this mindset and heartset, the focus becomes ensuring that the journey unfolds in the way your loved one wants, as much as possible. This might require you to stand firm to ensure that their wishes are met. I have had a couple of experiences with this – one as a loved one and one for a client.

The first occurrence happened once Mum was in the hospice. She had been there five days and had started to rapidly decline. It was very clear that she was absolutely where she needed to be. She had not been out of bed since the day she arrived and was not capable of holding her own weight anymore.

A psychologist who worked with Mum's oncologist had been in to see her and caught her at one of her most lucid moments, but by that point those were few and far between. Mum had been having quite a lot of paranoia about the staff harassing her and taking her things – which weren't being taken, just moved. It was bloody hard to see her like that, and it took some juggling of her medication to get it right.

This psychologist started talking about her having some chemo in the following week. The hospice did not have the capability to provide this, so it would have required moving her into an ambulance to be transferred to the oncology unit for the day and then coming back to the hospice, again via ambulance.

I absolutely knew this should not happen. Just getting Mum to the hospice from her home had been a massively tiring event for her, and one I did not want to see her subjected to again, let alone receiving chemo and taking a second ambulance ride. My Mum was not having any more treatment other than what she needed to keep her comfortable. She had made the choice some weeks earlier that she did not want any more chemo – she wanted quality of life.

This specialist did not even seem to realise Mum was at the end of her life. So I had to put the big girl panties on and stand firm. I stated that I had power of attorney and that the chemo treatment would not be happening. He tried to tell me that she was lucid enough to negate my authority. I advised him otherwise, and told him that he'd managed to speak with her in a lucid moment. I also know that even if he had asked Mum, she would not have agreed to any more chemo.

I think he got the message and backed off a bit, saying that we could review the situation again the following week. Mum died less than a week after this exchange – yes, she was at the end of her life.

The second situation was in relation to a client and her advance health directive. I had been working with her for about four months at this stage and had been meeting with her twice a week. Let's call her Sally (not her real name). Sally was in her early 60s and had advanced motor neuron disease (Lou Gehrig's disease, for my USA friends).

By the time I started visiting her in the residential care facility she now called home, she had a little head movement and a tiny bit of movement in one finger – that was all. Sally wished that she could end her life or that it could be ended for her. She was constantly in pain and discomfort and there was essentially no quality of life for her. Her prognosis at this stage was around six months. Sally was also getting chest infections every couple of months, which is common with this disease.

I had spoken to a few nurse friends about the disease in general and they all mentioned how chest infections and/or pneumonia can be a blessed release for these patients. It made me start to wonder what Sally had in her advance health directive around treatment for such occurrences.

I had a chat with her about it, and it turned out that her advance health directive did include a clause stating that she did not want to be treated with antibiotics when she was in the advanced stage of her disease – which she was. For the purposes of advance health directives in Queensland, 'advanced stage' is regarded as resulting in the patient having approximately less than 12 months to live. Long story short, the instructions in her advance health directive had either been forgotten or ignored as they continued to treat these chest infections.

I had a conversation with Sally, to ascertain whether it was still her wish not to receive treatment and what the implications of that might be for her. She was very clear that she didn't want treatment. She wanted her journey to end as soon as possible. So we made a bit of noise about the existence of her advance health directive, her wish not to be treated for chest infections, and how, in spite of this, she was still being treated.

Thankfully, the next time Sally got a chest infection, her wishes were honoured and she died a few weeks after all of this happened.

I don’t share this story to have a go at medical professionals. They are massively busy and often understaffed. This is, though, where you as the responsible person can ensure that your loved one’s wishes are met. You need to be crystal clear about them and then remind the medical staff, as needed, of what those wishes are.

This is one of the worst bits of the dying journey, but it’s also one of the most important. It’s when you get to stand up for your loved one and state what they want.

Chapter 9. Sharing with Kids

These days, kids are pretty switched on when it comes to things relating to dying and death. They're exposed to it much more than I remember when I was growing up – just look at the news and the nature of some video games. Dying and death are everywhere. Kids may also experience it directly through the loss of a pet.

I like to think that this is one area we have got better at handling since I was a kid. I remember that when an aunt and an uncle suicided a couple of years apart, it really wasn't discussed. And when my precious Grandpa died when I was seven, I wasn't allowed to go to his funeral, so I didn't get to say goodbye. Decades later, it is still on my mind.

The very best advice I can give you about children is to be honest within an age-appropriate context. It's about knowing your child and how much information to give and not give. And it's also about saying "I don't know" if you don't have an answer. Be honest. Kids have pretty good lie detectors and will pick it up if you're not being straight with them. This also allows you to show your kids that parents aren't all-knowing.

We all know that kids have pretty vivid imaginations. This is another reason I encourage you to be honest with the kids in your world, as otherwise they are probably going to make up something much more complex and potentially frightening than the truth.

Death is a natural part of the life cycle, and I truly believe that failing to include kids and talk to them about it is part of the reason we have so much trouble having conversations of this nature today.

I also beg of you not to say things like "Granny has gone to sleep now", as that may create issues for you around the kids going to sleep at some later stage. Likewise with "They've gone on a holiday" or "They went away". The next time someone special goes on a holiday, your kids may fear that they won't come back, or they may not wish to go on holiday themselves.

It's also important to explain, again with age-appropriate terminology, the differences between illnesses and the fact that some illnesses cannot always be healed. Be careful, too, around the word 'cancer' so that you don't plant the automatic assumption that all cancers will be fatal.

If your loved one is in some kind of care facility, be it a hospital, hospice residential care, or something else, allow your kids to visit them in this environment. This can go a long way towards removing some of the mystery, as kids won't necessarily have a frame of reference for where this loved one is living. Clearly, there will first need to be conversations about indoor voices (for little kids) and the fact that the loved one may not look well or may even been connected to medical equipment. Ensure that the kids are prepared as much as you can. You may find that your loved may feel lifted by having the kids visit.

It's worth letting kids know that some people may have different beliefs to them about what happens once someone physically dies, and that that's okay. Not everyone has to have the same beliefs, and this can start to create a sense of acceptance and tolerance of differences in beliefs.

I would also encourage you to be honest with your own emotions in front of kids. That goes for many different scenarios, not just this one. This allows your kids to know and understand that grief is part of the process and part of your experience.

Another aspect to consider is knowing that, depending on their relationship with your loved one, your kids will also mourn. So you should allow them to do so, and to find appropriate outlets for their grief. This could involve creating their own memory projects, drawing pictures, writing a poem or story, and so on.

It's also worthwhile, irrespective of their age, to make their kindergarten or school aware of what is going on. My daughter was in her final year of secondary school when my Mum died, and the help they provided to her was invaluable. They also made some allowances with some of her exams.

Conversations about death don't have to be really hard to have with kids. They often have a natural curiosity, and then it becomes about answering honestly based on your beliefs and understanding using age-appropriate language.

Chapter 10. Managing Family Drama

If ever there is a time conducive to family drama, a loved one's dying process is it. I'm going to take a slightly creative approach to this topic by using a recipe metaphor for how such drama comes to exist, and then provide you with some strategies for managing it.

Mixing Bowl – The Situation
Someone is actively dying. This could be someone precious in your world, or someone with whom you have issues – or it could be both.

If it is someone precious, there is anticipatory grief and loss. There is hurt. There is sadness. There are heightened emotions and sensitivity.

If it is someone with whom you have issues, a whole host of things might come up – impatience to get the issues resolved, a belief that the issues will never get resolved, or even guilt over the issues now that this person is dying. You may feel anger and possibly think that this person now has a 'get out of jail free' card in terms of resolving the issues. And these are just the top of the pile in terms of possibilities.

If this is someone precious in your world with whom you also have issues . . . well, look at the above and amplify the feelings even more.

Ingredient 1 – The Environment

According to the Grattan Institute report called "Dying Well" released in September 2014, 70% of people want to die at home, yet only about 14% do so. Approximately 54% die in hospitals and 32% die in residential care. So it is odds on there will be hospital, hospice, nursing home, or residential care involved at some stage, if not entirely. And these are environments that you will probably find uncomfortable, unless you work in them. An uncomfortable environment makes this whole situation a challenge from the start.

Ingredient 2 – Lack of Authority

If there is no enduring power of attorney, or equivalent document authorising someone to speak on behalf of the person who is dying when they are no longer able, there is the potential for conflict among loved ones who believe 'they know best'. The same situation can occur when there are multiple people given the same authority but who are not on the same page in terms of beliefs or understanding the dying person's wishes.

Ingredient 3 – Lack of Communication about Wishes

This ingredient follows on directly from the last one. As a society, we are not good at having discussions around end-of-life care and wishes. In fact, we avoid it like the plague.

I conducted a small survey in my business asking about various end-of-life planning matters. One of the questions was around advance health care planning and whether respondents had completed formal documentation on this. Only 8% had something completed. 37% didn't know what advance health care planning was. 18% had it on their to-do lists and 32% either didn't believe they needed it, didn't want to think about it or thought that is was just for the old and/or sick.

Again, according to the Grattan Institute report, a survey was undertaken in New South Wales residential aged care facilities, and only 5% of residents had documented advance health care directives, despite the fact that 90% of residents will die in that setting.

Even disregarding the ideal of something formal being in place, we are resistant to having conversations about what we want at the end of our lives. Some of this is also down to the resistance of medical professionals to have these conversations as well.

Ingredient 4 – Dysfunction

If this is an issue in any way, you can bet your bottom dollar that an awareness that someone within the dysfunctional dynamic is dying will amplify any issues – see the mixing bowl analogy above.

Ingredient 5 – Religious Beliefs

A situation with differing religious or spiritual beliefs has the potential for drama. This is also true if the person dying has had a change in their belief system as a result of their illness journey – as can often happen. Being advised of a terminal illness can sharply bring into focus what people do and don't believe and leave them deeply questioning. For others, it can completely strengthen their faith and belief, and provide them with great comfort.

The challenge comes when there are passionate differences and a lack of willingness to accept those differences. I know of one lady who no longer went along with her family's belief system as to religion and was not permitted to see her dying grandmother because of this.

Ingredient 6 – Personal Agenda

Take a moment and just think about how many times you have heard things like these:

- "I/We just want the best for them, which is . . . "
- "I/We just want them to have every opportunity to fight this"
- "I/We just want to look after them"
- "I/We just want them to make it to . . ."

Look at the start of each of those statements . . . "I/ We". I know of one 99-year-old lady whose family was desperate for her to live to the magic age of 100 and insisted that everything be done to ensure that she did, irrespective of what was going on for her. I heard of another situation where the family wanted to make sure that their loved one didn't die on a specific day as another family member was getting married, and they didn't want this person dying to spoil their wedding day.

If you place any or all of these ingredients into the mixing bowl of the situation, it doesn't take a genius to work out there are going to be issues. The intensity and number of issues will simply vary.

The 'why' behind all of this is actually pretty simple – and extremely uncomfortable for some people. The focus is not squarely on the person who is dying and their wishes. It's all about everyone else. This may sound harsh, but the reality is that we have the opportunity to sort out our stuff separate to the person who is dying, and certainly after they are gone if necessary. The person dying does not have that luxury. This is a time when every decision made should be about the person who is dying and their wishes – that's it.

So how do we prevent drama? These are some steps:

- As discussed in earlier chapters, ensure that there is a legal document in place giving authority to someone to make decisions on behalf of the person who is dying when they are no longer able to do so. Again, this does not need to be a family member. The dying person should pick someone who has an intimate understanding of what they want, and who also has the capacity to jump up and down and stand their ground on their behalf if needed.
- Make sure the wishes of the dying are known – preferably through a formal document if not just having the conversations. This makes it easier for medical staff as well.

If you are in a drama-filled situation with a loved one who is dying, try these:

- If possible, see whether everyone involved can undertake this exercise on their own. Set aside at least 15 minutes for this, possibly much longer. Find somewhere quiet and without distractions. Imagine that you have been diagnosed with a terminal illness or have become aware that you are going to die within a really short space of time – less than a month.

Connect deeply to that knowledge. Then start with thinking about all the little practicalities that need to be addressed and think about these questions:

- Do you have current legal paperwork in place?
- Do any kids or pets need to be considered?
- Are there enough assets in your estate to cover any debts? If not, what will happen?
- Are there bank accounts that need to be amalgamated, closed or changed?
- What passwords do you need to communicate?
- What about all your social media?
- If you are employed, are there matters relating to your work that others will need to know or understand?
- Do you have any possessions you wouldn't want others to find? What do you do about those?

These questions are only the very surface of everything that needs to be addressed. You'll see this if you allow your mind to wander through all the different aspects of your life. Hopefully after this exercise there will be a shift in everyone's thought processes to start thinking differently and trying to understand things from the perspective of the person who is dying. It is confronting.

- The focus must be solely on the person who is dying and their wishes – perhaps remind everyone of this.
- In interactions between loved ones, be mindful that this is a challenging time for everyone involved and remember that sometimes things are said in the heat of the moment that are not necessarily intended.
- If there are vocal fights between loved ones in the presence of the person who is dying, get them to take it elsewhere.
- Be respectful of others' beliefs, even if they are different to yours.
- Remember that loved ones will have the chance to sort out their issues after the person who is dying has died – but the dying person won't.

- Respectfully speak your truth. If it is ignored, disrespected or otherwise discarded, find a way to deal with this in your own way – counselling, exercise, meditating, whatever. Many support services are available for loved ones, so seek support if you need it.

Family drama and having a loved one who is terminally ill do not need to go hand-in-hand. Drama can be managed and even avoided, provided the starting place is a genuine focus on the needs and wishes of the person who is dying.

Chapter 11. Healing and Resolving Issues

The context of healing takes on a whole different light once we start talking about someone who has a terminal illness or disease, or knows that their life is going to be shortened. It ceases to be about a cure or physical recovery. It becomes about healing on different levels.

How do we get into situations where there is healing is needed? In the words of 10CC (yes, I'm showing my age), "Communication is the problem to the answer". So very often communication, whether it be ineffective or nonexistent, creates a much bigger issue than that which would otherwise exist.

Part of this problem is how we communicate. Stop and take a look around your world for a little while. I've done this and I see people talking *at* each other rather than *with* or *to* each other. And that's if the other party is actually listening, not checking their phone, scrolling through social media, or multitasking in other ways. We seem to have lost the art of effective communication.

Another aspect of the communication problem is the blame game. We have become very skilled at avoiding taking responsibility for ourselves and our thoughts, our words and our actions. This is encouraged by the litigious society that we have become. I could wax lyrical about all of this, but I think you get the message that effective communication is a real issue for us these days.

The challenge then becomes, how do you resolve issues and create healing in an environment that is already highly emotionally charged? One guiding question, for me, must be answered before anything else. In the effort to create healing, for either you, your dying loved one or both of you, ask yourself this question: “Will or could what I am proposing to do cause more pain?” If the answer is yes, find another way.

The main way that comes to mind involves seeking forgiveness directly from another person for something done or not done. It is perfectly normal to want to redress a situation, apologise and seek forgiveness. However, if this is likely to cause more pain to the other party involved, I would strongly suggest finding another way to make peace. If remorse is genuine, is the seeking of forgiveness truly to make the wronged one feel better, or is it perhaps more about the person seeking forgiveness wanting to feel better? Yes, I’m getting a little bit in-the-face here.

Whoever is seeking to redress a situation, I would suggest that working with someone external to the situation could be very beneficial – e.g., a counsellor or minister. Whether it's you seeking to heal an issue with your dying loved one or it's them trying to resolve issues before they die, it really is worth taking the time to consider the possible impacts of proposed actions. An independent party can be invaluable in this scenario.

Healing can occur in a number of different ways. These are just some of them:

- Does the situation need to be addressed at all? For example, in the grand scheme of life, is it really a serious issue, or is it something that perhaps got a bit exaggerated? And given that a loved one is dying, does it now really matter?

  I had this happen with my Dad. I wouldn't say we had been estranged, but we had certainly not been anywhere near close to each other for some time. The moment he told me that he had cancer and only had 6–12 months to live, everything else seem to fade into insignificance. The five-and-a-half months that we got to share were so incredibly precious. There were more "I love you" comments shared between us than there had ever been.

What became important was creating special memories and sharing quality time together in whatever time we had left. My Dad died back in 2000, and to this day I am still very thankful for that opportunity.

- Can healing be undertaken through a heartfelt conversation in which you each gently, lovingly and compassionately share your experiences? This needs to happen with the intent that all parties involved genuinely wish to resolve the situation – otherwise it isn't going to work. Again, if need be, utilise an independent person to assist and help facilitate the discussion.

- Can healing be achieved within oneself without involved the other party or parties at all? In this scenario, I am suggesting perhaps writing down all that you are feeling in a journal or letter that will never be posted.
- Can healing be undertaken through working with a counsellor of some sort who can help you work through the issues?

- Can healing happen through you forgiving yourself for whatever happened or didn't happen and your participation in it?

Healing of this nature can also happen on an energetic level. When genuine healing is the goal, that result can be achieved through a number of modalities – I think specifically of EFT (Emotional Freedom Technique or 'tapping'), hypnotherapy and guided spirit/soul work in a meditative state.

I worked with a client who was shortly to lose her ability to speak. She was also conscious that she wasn't really good at expressing directly to those most precious to her what she wanted to say. So we made some audio recordings of the messages she wanted to give to them. Each was less than two minutes long and they were filled with love. She made me promise to give these to her loved ones at her funeral, and that's what happened. Those messages of love provided so much healing and are there to be treasured forever.

What's important to remember is that the goal here is to create peace, not open wounds that may have already healed or aggravate wounds that are still raw. This can be a beautiful time with the opportunity to create much healing, but the intent must be pure, for the best and highest good of all involved.

Chapter 12. Being Open to Gifts and Blessings

This may sound truly bizarre to you, but knowing that your loved one's life is going to be shortened can provide many gifts and blessings, if you are open to receiving them.

The first prerequisite, of course, is the actual knowing. My beloved hubby Reid found his Dad dead in his unit. His Dad had not been particularly unwell, and we'd certainly had no indication that his time was drawing to a close. I watched my beloved absolutely racked with pain, as he and his Dad were close. They had no unresolved issues at all. My beloved simply didn't get that final opportunity to say all that he wanted to say or do what he may have wanted to do.

I had a similar situation with my precious Aunty Maggs, my Mum's identical twin. I was blessed to have two Mums, and Maggs often referred to me as the daughter she didn't have. Maggs had had heart surgery with some complications, but she was seemingly on the road to recovery. The last time I had spoken to her, she had sounded better than she had in a long time. But then she had a massive heart attack and died just a few days after leaving hospital.

It was a total shock. I can remember thinking that I would call her the afternoon she died and decided not to as I knew they were having visitors over for my Uncle's birthday that weekend and I thought she would be tired. She died that evening. Not everyone gets to know their time is coming to an end.

Think back to the survey I mentioned in Chapter 5. Again, this is the golden opportunity to work on reducing the regret aspect of your grieving experience. Attitude is an incredibly powerful force in our lives and we get to choose what our attitude will be. I am not for a minute denying the sadness that is a natural and expected part of the experience; it just doesn't need to be the nature of the entire experience.

I need to quote my big sister here. This gem of hers appeared in a publication for a cancer organisation and while it was written from her perspective as someone living with cancer, it holds true for us as the loved ones sharing the journey as well.

"Your greatest support, your greatest strength and the aspect you have the most influence over is your attitude – the way you think about your experience. Your thinking will influence your journey. I'm not for a second saying that you always have to be happy and jolly – that would be to live a phony life. Just be real. Enjoy the good days; continue to love yourself on the no-so-good days. Be alert or aware of how your thinking, your attitude, influences your experience. Above all, listen to yourself, love yourself, accept yourself. Know deep within that whether you have cancer or not, whether you are well or not, know that you are loveable and acceptable."

Liz Stone (aka my sister Bess)

I received so many gifts from sharing the end journeys with not only my loved ones, but also my clients. One thing that I have found is that the dying have no capacity for BS. They much prefer honesty, and that allows for some phenomenal conversations – again, if you allow it.

Lastly, be open to gifts and blessings from the most unexpected people and areas of your life. The people that came into my life, or who stepped up their presence in my life through the various experiences with my loved ones, were truly nothing short of spectacular in terms of what they brought and how they helped. Likewise, there were also some who weren't there as I would have hoped, and those were blessings in other ways.

This is a journey and an experience in which the little things really aren't little at all. Those gifts, those blessings, carry the most significance and I consider them to be the most precious. Those vanilla slices that I shared with Mum? I will never forget that.

Chapter 13. Sometime It Sucks - Getting Help

I truly wish that I could say to you that you won't have any bad times. But I can't, and you know it. Even with a positive attitude and looking for the gifts, there will be times when this journey just sucks big time. The benefit of having a positive attitude and looking for the gifts means that these times don't last as long and don't feel as hard as they otherwise can.

I remember the day Mum moved into the hospice as being one of the hardest. The palliative care team rang and confirmed that they had a bed for her and asked if we wanted an ambulance to take her there. I said "Yes, please", as I was not sure how else I would have gotten Mum out into the wheelchair, into the car, and out again at the hospice. By this stage, her bone cancer had advanced to such a degree that her frame had started to collapse in on itself and Mum was not able to carry her own weight. We'd had a lot of challenges the previous night just getting her to and from the toilet.

The ambulance officers were fantastic about getting Mum moved. They were able to get her into the wheelchair and then onto their gurney just outside the front of Mum's unit. My daughter was able to ride in the ambulance with her and I was to follow behind in the car with Mum's things. Mum had been saving her brand new, pink, soft, fluffy dressing gown, for when she went into the hospice and she looked so snug and warm in it.

While they were getting Mum settled in the ambulance, I quickly gathered the last bits and pieces and then just stood and bawled my eyes out for a few moments. I could have so easily collapsed in a heap and cried my heart out for all eternity at that moment. My heart was completely breaking. I knew that she was leaving her unit for the last time and that this was the start of the next and last phase. Even typing this long after the fact, I can feel the tears welling up again.

The worst part was that I couldn't give in to all that I was feeling at that moment as I had to gather everything and then drive behind the ambulance to the hospice. I wasn't completely sure of where I was going. I am very thankful that I had the ambulance to follow as I was certainly not focussed on driving or watching where I was going.

The upside was that I knew life would be much easier for Mum in the hospice. They could provide a level of care that I couldn't and had the equipment that would make everything easier – things that we just couldn't have fit into Mum's little one-bedroom unit. But in that moment, it was all I could do to just keep going.

You've no doubt heard the saying about taking things 'a day at a time'. But sometimes a day is way too long. Sometimes it needs to be an hour or even a minute. Sometimes it's about taking one deep breath . . . and then another . . . and then another . . . and that's your only focus in those moments. Taking deep breaths so that you can keep going a little while longer, so that you can allow yourself to collapse in a heap later. The only way to navigate these times is to be super-gentle with yourself. Know that 'this, too, shall pass', even if at that moment it feels like your world is going to implode.

You also need to know that if you are the closest person to your loved one, you will most likely be the safe space for them to be authentic about their experience. This can also mean that you are the safe space for them to express their anger. And it sucks!

If this happens to you, please be aware that although it may feel like it, their anger is not being directed at you and it may not even be about you. It can be about their frustration, it can be about their awareness of their reality and it can be about the challenges that they are experiencing. This was particularly so with my Mum. There were a couple of times where I felt like I was a little kid in trouble again – at home it was never a case of 'wait until your father gets home'. Mum was the disciplinarian when I was growing up.

One of these experiences was huge. Four days before Mum died, we actually thought she was going to die. She was really out of it. Her breathing was very shallow, she was pale and clammy and she truly was not present. I was so glad that my hubby, daughter and another family member were flying in that afternoon as I thought we were down to hours. Mum hadn't really eaten anything on the day before and she certainly was not up to eating that day. I just sat quietly with her, holding her hand and stroking it. Silent tears were falling in a steady stream down my face . . . my Mum was dying.

I had gotten close with one of the nurses in particular and he had been on duty that morning. When he left that afternoon, I asked him when he was next on. He said that was two days away and we hugged and said our goodbyes as neither of us expected Mum to still be alive by then.

We all finally left the hospice that day and went home, waiting for the phone call telling us to come back in. Mum had said that she wanted any of us that wanted to be, to be with her when she went if it was possible.

The phone call never came that night.

I wanted to get in early the next morning and see how she was. I was so totally unprepared for what greeted us when we walked in. Mum was sitting up in bed and had a go at me, asking me what had taken me so long to get there. She was quite angry that I had not come earlier. I told her that it was not even 9am. Gotta love getting an ass kick from someone you expected to be at death's door – not!

Another relative came in and got kisses and cuddles. Didn't that just suck! I got in trouble and they got all the love! Mum had totally rallied and could not have been further from the patient she had been the day before. I was glad others had seen her the day before, as I truly don't think they would have believed me if they had not seen for themselves compared to how she was on that morning.

Next thing I knew she was eating porridge and drinking some juice. 'Who are you and what have you done with my mother?' I wondered. I don't think I can accurately convey how challenging this was from an emotional perspective. I had steeled myself for Mum's death and yet there she was, sitting up and looking relatively healthy. And I felt like I was like a little kid getting in trouble again. And of course, then I felt guilty that I wasn't happy and ecstatic that she looked so good. That experience was one massive emotional roller coaster.

I talked with her GP later in the day. Mum worked with this doctor for over ten years, so she was much more to Mum than just her GP. She said that Mum's reaction was not uncommon and that "they always hurt those they love the most". So just be aware that this may be a part of your experience, too.

This is where getting help comes into play. Call on your loved ones who will allow you to just be, call on counsellors, and anyone else who you feel can help you out. If things feel like they are becoming too overwhelming, please seek assistance. There are always multiple avenues from which you can obtain assistance – you may just need to ask. This is part of taking care of yourself so that you can continue to take care of your loved one. It's knowing yourself well enough to recognise that you need either a small time out or you really do need some external support to get you through this experience.

There is absolutely no shame in needing support. I'm going to say that again – *there is absolutely no shame in needing support.* This is one of the biggies in life in terms of challenging emotions – and this might be a newsflash to you – but you are having a human experience. That brings with it a whole host of emotions.

Once again, we are back to authenticity and vulnerability. Vulnerability is a way to build connection to and with others. And if you can't be authentic to your experience, expressing your vulnerability and how you may be struggling, when you are sharing the end journey with a loved one, then when can you?

This is someone precious in your world. You will have anticipatory grief. And it's okay to feel all of that and for it to sometimes feel crap! Because it is.

As I mentioned, if need be, ask for help and seek help.

Chapter 14. It's Okay to Laugh

One of the things I need you to know here and now is that this experience does not need to be totally dark and heavy. Yes – shock! horror! – you are allowed to laugh.

It's been said that sometimes the only choices we have are to laugh or cry, and sometimes you might have had enough of crying. Humour can be a fantastic way to release the emotional pressure valve and can provide the opportunity for you and others to take a much-needed breather.

When I went down to be with my Mum in her last weeks, one of the first things I said to her was, "You get one use of playing the 'I'm dying' card to get you into doing something or out of doing something, so use it wisely." My Mum absolutely cracked up laughing! I can imagine that to some people, this would have seemed very inappropriate and even disrespectful. For us, it was authentic to the nature of the relationship we shared.

While my family was gathered around Dad's bed at the hospice after we got the call that he was probably down to mere hours remaining, we all recalled a number of precious memories that resulted in laughter. The gift was in the shared communion of the experience. At this stage Dad was not conscious, but I like to think that he heard the laugher and it made his journey that little bit easier.

When my sister Bess was going through her chemotherapy, like most people, she lost her hair. Her comment? "Well, at least I don't have to get my eyebrows plucked now."

Humour can acknowledge some of the crappy aspects of the journey in ways that aren't quite as confronting as they otherwise might be. Provided that it's not malicious in intent, humour is a powerful tool in your kit that enables you to navigate this journey.

And with thanks to http://darkclass.wordpress.com/2010/11/05/macabre-jokes/ , this one appealed to my sense of humour:

Two men were walking home after a night in the tavern and decided to take a shortcut through the cemetery to get to their homes quicker. In the middle of the cemetery they were startled by a tap-tap-tapping noise coming from the misty shadows. Trembling with fear, they found an old man with a hammer and chisel, chipping away at one of the headstones.

"Good gracious, Sir," one of them said after catching his breath, "You scared us half to death — we thought you were a ghost! What are you doing working here so late at night?"

"Those fools!" the old man grumbled. "They misspelled my name!"

There is a reason for the saying 'laughter is the best medicine'. Without getting too technical, the short version is that when we are smiling and laughing, the body releases endorphins, which are the feel-good chemicals in the brain. Other activities such as exercise and sex can also release endorphins. These have been known to block pain – and the best bit is that you can trick your brain! The brain does not register the difference between a fake smile or laugh and a real one. If you start smiling or laughing, it will start releasing endorphins and you may just find yourself smiling or laughing for real. Smiles and laughs are also contagious, in the very best way.

So go ahead, allow yourself to laugh. Allow yourself to find some humour in what can be the crappiness of your experience and just allow it to flow.

Chapter 15. Creating Sacred Space

As I have mentioned numerous times, this is a sacred experience that you are sharing with your loved one. In this and the next chapter, I will cover the aspects of both creating and holding sacred space. These are the some of the practical, simple, yet very energetically powerful processes that you can undertake. Both of these processes are vitally important, particularly as your loved one enters the actively dying stage. Through these processes, you can create an environment that starts to energetically and vibrationally match that towards which your loved one is going – the Divine to which they are returning home. This is the realm of pure love and peace, and it can be created in the earth realm as well.

Creating Sacred Space

One of the most important aspects of the dying person's end journey is having a peaceful, sacred space in which they can die. Creating a sacred space allows for the promotion of peace and gentleness and defines the area around your loved one as being truly special. And it's not difficult to create.

For the most part, it doesn't matter whether they are at home, in a hospital, hospice or nursing home – the main exception to this rule is the use of open flame candles, which most hospitals won't allow and which can't be used near medical oxygen.

Creating a sacred space begins with intent, so take a few moments to hold the intent of transforming the space. If you're in a hospital or other public facility, do curtains need to be drawn to form a physical boundary? Does a note need to be placed on a door to indicate that this is a sacred space?

Then comes de-cluttering. Take away any mess, any rubbish and anything that is superfluous to what is needed or wanted in the space. Ensure that you leave anything that is precious to your loved one. This is about what your loved one wants and needs.

Next up is cleaning – both the space and your loved one. Does the room need cleaning or airing? Is there tidying to be done? If so, ensure that it is done discreetly and with minimal disruption to your loved one. Do flowers need freshening? The sense of smell can be particularly heightened at this time, especially if your loved one has undergone chemo. Be mindful of this.

Does the linen need changing? Does your loved one need a wash? I don't know about you, but have a think about when you go to the hairdresser's . . . for me, the absolute best part is the scalp massage that comes with the hair wash. Would a gentle and loving wash be soothing for your loved one? I remember how effective the nurses were at Mum's hospice at changing the linen, washing her and changing her bedclothes with ease and almost no disruption to Mum.

Are there any special clothes or blankets/rugs that your loved one would like to have? My Mum had a beautiful Pashmina given to her by some loved ones that she wore in the hospice. I found some super-soft socks when we bought her brand new soft and fluffy dressing gown . . . she kept these for the hospice. Think about when you go somewhere special – you dress up. This is no different. After she had died, we sent her off wearing these things as they were very special to her.

Add some candles or imitation candles as bright light can be harsh. If overhead lighting is needed, see if it can be dimmed to soften it. If your loved one is agreeable, place appropriate essential oils in an electric burner or diffuser, remembering again that the sense of smell can be heightened at this time. Be aware of any smells that are either pleasing or unpleasant to your loved one. I have a little story for you on this topic . . .

When I walked back into Mum's room at the hospice after she had died, it looked so beautiful. The staff had done a wonderful job. A patchwork quilt had been placed on her bed, all of her personal items were in the drawers, the flowers that had been clustered on the sideboard were now spread around her room and some imitation candles were glowing softly on the bedside table. She looked so incredibly peaceful. As I walked in, I had a chuckle – the electric oil burner was going and it had some lavender essential oil in it. Mum was allergic to lavender. I can remember saying, "Well, it's just as well you're gone as that lavender would be an issue!" Back to the laughter thing again; yes, humour can bring some comfort.

Play some music – either music that has special significance for your loved one or just gentle new age or nature sounds. Something soothing to quietly play in the background is generally good. Ensure that the volume is kept low and that the music is not harsh. Again, this is about creating an environment of peace and calm for your loved one.

It's been said that hearing is the last sense to leave the physical body, and I believe this to be true. You can find many reports of people who have had near-death experiences and who are able to recount conversations when they were supposedly comatose or clinically dead. If you talk to any number of experienced palliative nurses, they will share with you many examples of seeing changes in their patients when loved ones speak.

In the book *The Harp and The Ferryman* by Helen Cox and Peter Roberts, numerous examples are given of the changes in physical experiences such as heart rates and breathing when Peter undertakes his work. Peter is a music thanatologist –someone who utilises harp and voice for the dying and their loved ones with specific music.

For me, having this belief that our loved ones can hear us right to the very end brings a level of comfort, and it also brings opportunity. It means that final loving words can be said and that sounds can be used to bring comfort to our loved ones at the end – as in Peter's music.

The most important part of creating sacred space is acting a bit like the police. This sacred space is to be absolutely honoured by everyone who comes to visit your loved one. This is not the space for talking about your loved one as though they are already dead. This is not the place for family squabbles, discussions about the estate, or personal agendas. This is the place for honouring your loved one – for loving thoughts, words and deeds. This is the place for softness and gentleness and love.

Another thing to consider with sacred space is that at the physical end of life, the spirit can sometimes need some space to finally withdraw. I think this is why you hear so many stories of people dying when they are alone while loved ones have quickly gone to the toilet or to get something to eat or drink. My sister Bess instinctively knew this. She had said to all of us that she wanted to die on her own, with only her caregiver present. At the time, that was bloody hard for all of us as loved ones, remembering that we had had the beautiful experience around Dad. I know I felt hurt and so did some other family members. It somehow felt like there was a lack of love. With what I've learned since then, I now know differently.

Having people constantly around and sometimes even touching can anchor our loved ones here in our physical reality and make it hard for them to withdraw. I experienced this with a client and her beautiful family. This lady was in her 90s and had birthed ten children. Nine were still alive and the life force in this woman was incredibly powerful. This family displayed the mostly extraordinary love and affection, with no discord. I have never seen anything like it, especially in such a large family.

I was called in to assist as it was clear this lady was at the end of her journey and there was a struggle. When I went into her room, two or three of her kids were touching her, with another half a dozen or so in the room and the same number outside. The energy in the room was incredibly high. The lights were on, music was playing and in some ways it was sensory overload.

I energetically connected with this beautiful lady and it became very clear that physically she was absolutely spent, but this life force still pulsed through her. I had a quiet conversation with some of her kids and commented, "It's such a challenge balancing wanting and needing to demonstrate your love for your Mum and allowing her the space for her spirit to withdraw". They got it in a heartbeat. The lights were turned down, as was the music, and they pulled back a little. I worked on an energetic level and created a sort of bubble around her as well.

I spoke with one of her kids outside and suggested that maybe only have two to three in the room at any one time. She agreed. This precious lady left her physical body around 12 hours later with just three of her children present.

This is a powerful example of sacred space.

Crystals

Crystals can be a powerful part of creating the right energetic vibration. I have detailed below some of the ones I use when working with clients. Most of these just called to me. With thanks to Judy Hall's *The Crystal Bible* for the meanings:

Green Obsidian

Green obsidian opens and purifies the heart and throat chakras. It removes hooks and ties from other people and protects against repetition.

Dalmatian Jasper

Jasper is known as the 'supreme nurturer'. It sustains and supports during times of stress, and brings tranquility and wholeness. It is a stone of protection from nightmares, depression and negative thinking.

Mangano Calcite

Mangano calcite is a heart crystal in contact with the angelic realm. A stone of forgiveness, it releases fear and grief that keep the heart trapped in the past, bringing in unconditional love. Mangano calcite's loving energy gently dissolves resistance.

Blue Calcite

Blue calcite is a gentle stone for recuperation and relaxation. It lowers blood pressure and dissolves pain on all levels. Gently soothing the nerves and lifting anxieties, it releases negative emotions.

Lepidolite

Lepidolite is a stone of transition and gentle change. It is a calming stone that soothes sleep disturbances and emotional stress, bringing deep emotional healing.

(This is one of my favourites – I work with it personally and professionally heaps!)

Angelite

Angelite is a stone that represents peace and brotherhood. It enhances telepathic communication and enables out-of-body journeys. It also provides protection for the environment or the body. It creates a deep feeling of peace and tranquillity and facilitates the re-birthing process.

Clear Quartz

Quartz is the most powerful healing and energy amplifier. It raises energy to the highest possible level. It is a master healer and can be used for any condition. It brings the body into balance.

Amethyst

Amethyst is an extremely powerful and protective stone with a high spiritual vibration. It balances out highs and low, promoting emotional centreing. Alleviating sadness and grief, it supports coming to terms with loss. It cleanses the aura and transmutes negative energy. It is helpful for people about to make the transition through death.

As I mentioned, these are just some of the crystals I use. If your loved one has some particular favourite it can also be used.

Ceremonies and Rituals

If appropriate, some sacred ceremonies or rituals can be held in this place which can be as simple as loved ones gathering around, holding hands and sharing treasured memories. If need be, such ceremonies can involve giving your loved one permission to die and letting them know that while you will miss them, you will all be okay.

Ceremonies don't need to be steeped in eons of doctrine, unless of course they are in alignment with your loved one's spiritual or religious beliefs. If they are, then absolutely include the time-honoured experiences that are part of their belief system.

For everyone else, keep it simple. Intent is the main power in all of this work. If your loved one has a birthday during their experience, or someone special to them does, still celebrate. Yes, it might be a slightly lower-key celebration than usual, but celebrate. When my Dad was in the hospice, we weren't sure if he would make it to Christmas. So while he was still lucid, we had a family picnic/early Christmas celebration in the grounds of the hospice. It was a fabulous day and I was so glad that we did this. There were lots of laughs and corny jokes (as usual), and treasured memories were made. Christmas up to that time had always been a wonderfully huge, noisy and precious family event and this in some ways was no different. Dad was still physically present by the time Christmas arrived, but he was not conscious.

Here's another thing you can do . . . place Himalayan salt in bowls in the corner of the room to absorb negativity. You just need to make sure that it is changed regularly.

In short, do whatever you can to ensure that the place where your loved one is dying is honoured as a sacred space.

Chapter 16. Holding Sacred Space

I don't think it's possible for me to overemphasise just how powerful and precious the experience of holding sacred space can be – for both you and your loved one. This concept is not well-known to many people these days, and it is certainly not something that is actively encouraged. Yet its capacity and potential are truly limitless.

The energy of holding sacred space is the same as that of meditation and prayer, and its benefits and potential capacity for change have been well documented over the ages. I want to highlight one example.

In Washington in the summer of 1993, a scientifically controlled two-month trial was conducted to show how easy and simple it was to reduce crime and social stress by using meditation. The aim was to create a reduction of more than 20% in the crime rate. The police chief at the time was quoted as saying that the only way this would happen was if 20 inches of snow fell – and remember, this was in the summer.

Over the period of the study, between 800 and 4,000 meditators took part. The final result was that there was a maximum reduction in crime over the period of 23.3%. Yes, a massive impact.

Holding sacred space is an act of pure and unconditional love. It involves connecting deeply and with pure intent with whatever you call the Divine – God, Spirit, Source, the Universe – whatever is appropriate for you within the context of your beliefs.

It means completely disconnecting from what you believe to be important and focussing all of your attention and love on your loved one, intending that their experience will be for the best and highest good of all concerned. It means removing judgement from your experience and allowing yourself to be infused with pure and unconditional love for your loved one. When your mind starts to wander (and it's a fairly safe bet that it will), gently bringing your focus back to being on your loved one.

You can visualise your loved one being wrapped in a cloud like the energy of pure and unconditional love, in which they are fully protected and supported.

It doesn't matter whether you do this for five minutes or five hours. What's important is the power of your intention.

This can be done while physically in the presence of your loved one or it can be done remotely. I do this a lot for people anywhere in the world and there is always a positive, gentle and loving impact.

This is also a gift that you give to yourself. It creates a space in which you sit in pure love, and it is impossible for you to hold this for someone else and not receive it into your own being. For love is a deeply connecting force.

This act reconnects us with each other at the deepest level, and in doing so we are reminded that there is no separation from one another or from that which we know as Source, which is the basis of all pure and unconditional love.

Holding sacred space is also an act of allowing, of not forcing any particular action, outcome or process, of releasing expectation and trusting that in the grand scheme of things, events are unfolding exactly as they are meant to be – that is all is perfect just as it is.

Now I know that can be a really challenging concept, particularly if your loved one is really struggling with their journey. We have a very limited field of vision, and of course we have no conscious knowledge of our own soul contract, let alone that of another. The very best you can do for your loved one is to hold this sacred space around them which is based in pure and unconditional love. As mentioned previously, this vibration, this energy is in alignment with the energy of where they are going, so it makes sense that it makes that transition easier.

The actual process for holding sacred space is simply to get yourself comfortable, settle into your heart and focus all of your conscious awareness on to your loved one. This can be done in either a meditative or prayerful state, whichever is more appropriate or comfortable for you.

Just allow yourself to be with this process, and as mentioned earlier, when your mind starts to wander, gently bring your focus back. If you are physically with your loved one, it may help when you are first doing this to be gently touching them, holding their hand or in some other way. Check with them as to what feels right for them.

I have created a very special meditation piece to assist you in this process. It is called the Holding Sacred Space meditation and can be purchased through my Spiritual Palliative Care website. The music is absolutely spectacular in terms of its gentleness and it is uplifting without being too ethereal. Christopher Lloyd Clarke worked his magic in creating this piece. I then blended the music with words to guide you through the process. I also energetically infused the recording with my connection to the Divine and pure and unconditional love, both for you and your loved one. It is designed to support all of you and to hold space for you as you hold space for your loved one.

Holding sacred space is something that you can do as often as you like and wherever you are. I wouldn't recommend it while driving or anything that needs your conscious attention, but wherever you can stop and focus on your loved one, you can hold this sacred space for yourself and for them. Do not doubt for a second that there is immense power in this experience.

One of my clients was in a particularly agitated and distressed state one day. Even her favourite nurses were struggling with her, and she was really quite upset. I arrived to see her for our normal visit and she did not want to see me. So I chose to spend some time holding some sacred space for both her and her nursing staff on a remote basis. All I said to the nurses was that I would do some energetic work.

When I went back a few days later, I happened to see one of the same nurses. She looked at me and said straightaway, "What did you do?" I asked her what she meant, and she told me that this lady's attitude, energy and behaviour changed very dramatically and quickly after my visit. She said that she had become very calm and peaceful and there was nothing that the nursing staff could attribute it to. They had not given her any sedatives, nor was there any other outer reason they could see for the change. She also stated that the nursing staff had also felt a calmness come over them at the same time this was happening for their patient . . . not after, as you might imagine. The nurse told me the difference had been absolutely staggering. I told her that I had done some energetic work , as promised, and was just holding them all in a sacred space of pure and unconditional love. The nurse said that whatever I had done, I should keep doing it! Of course I do, and it's something that I freely encourage others to do as well.

I had another client who was in a shared room in a hospice (which is, incidentally, one of my pet peeves). I saw this lady over the period of about three weeks in this place, and during that time there would have been at least six or so other people who shared the room with her as they ended their physical journeys in this lifetime. This lady was very much at peace with her own journey, but the energy within the room when I went to see her was often not peaceful and sometimes felt almost distressing.

The most powerful thing I could do for he was to transform the energy of the room into that of peace and unconditional love. So I did. A lot of the time we worked together we did not speak much at all. I would just sit quietly at her bedside, gently holding her hand and expanding my heart space energy to transform that of the room's energy. I wish I could accurately convey the nature of this experience, but there truly are no words that could ever do it justice. You'll just have to trust me when I say that it was a massively powerful experience and created the most beautiful space in which she could be.

Holding sacred space is an absolutely precious gift and one that is not hard – anyone can do it, it just requires a sole focus for an intense period of time to surround your loved one with pure and unconditional love.

Chapter 17. Dignity Therapy

I want to share a process with you that is a powerful tool for capturing information about your loved one. It's called Dignity Therapy, and it was created by Dr Harvey Max Chochinov, a palliative care doctor in Canada. He created it to provide a way to capture the life journey of your loved one from an experiential perspective, not just a chronological one. It's a life review conversation.

In an ideal world, we wouldn't need to have life review conversations. Instead, we would all be communicating with each other authentically and discussing what is and has been important to us. In an ideal world, we would have soulful connections on a much more regular basis.

But of course, we know that our world is not ideal in these terms.

Having a life review conversation is a powerful process that can offer much healing. It is much more than creating a eulogy, which is often just a chronological catalogue of a person's experiences and roles.

Dignity Therapy focuses more on the feelings and emotions attached to those experiences and roles. The nature of the questions is more experiential, and they enable us to understand much more about our loved one than the outer basics. A life review conversation allows for an expanded view of our loved one.

Some of the questions asked in it are:

- When did you feel most alive?
- Are there particular things that you would want your family to know about you, and are there particular things you would want them to remember?
- What are the most important roles you have played in your life (e.g., family roles, vocational roles, community service roles)? Why were they so important to you, and what do you think you accomplished within those roles?
- Are there particular things that you feel need to be said to your loved ones or things that you would want to take the time to say once again?

In some ways it does make sense to leave off creating something like this until we know a loved one is on their end journey, but not all of us are granted that gift. When I was training in this therapy, I did some practice runs with a couple of my friends – neither of whom are on their end journeys. Both felt that they gained great value from the experience, particularly if something was to suddenly happen to them. One of them even said that this should be done alongside with preparing one's will.

I believe the power in this therapy lies in understanding our loved one's experience from their perspective. It provides an opportunity for our loved ones (or even ourselves) to express what's most important and what emotional significance various experiences have had.

This is particularly important if the dying loved one is a parent. We generally have a pretty two-dimensional perspective of our parent's lives, particularly before we came along. We may know of their experiences and roles, but we may have no concept of what it all meant to them on an emotional level. It's a bit like thinking about your parents having sex – you know that they had to have had it, but that's it. (Okay, so maybe it's not exactly like sex between our folks, as we probably don't *want* to know more about that!)

Dignity Therapy fills out the picture of our loved ones as fully functioning, emotional human beings, not just people fulfilling certain roles. This allows for deeper connections and, in the case of experiences that have been traumatic, it can facilitate healing. I know of one situation where there had been no contact between a lady and her daughters in over ten years. Through this process, contact was resumed and their differences were resolved prior to this lady's death. What a gift for all concerned!

This process does need to be undertaken with someone who is trained in the therapy or has counselling experience to ensure that any issues that may arise are handled appropriately.

I believe there is much value is completing this process because quite simply it facilitates a deeper connection between people and I am all for anything that creates that. If you are interested in learning more about Dignity Therapy or your loved one would like to create their own legacy document, please contact me through the Spiritual Palliative Care website.

Chapter 18. False Hope

I would like to address another aspect of the dying one's journey, and that is the issue of Ffalse hope. When we think of hope and relate it to illness or disease, many people directly associate that with hope of a cure or recovery and of returning to full physical wellness. However, in the end-of-life context, hope must, by necessity, take on a very different form.

First, though, we need to explore hope on a deeper level. According to dictionary.com, the definition of hope is 'the feeling that what is wanted can be had or that events will turn out for the best'. And this, of course, is wholly subjective – what we want or consider to be the best could be very different to the perspective of someone else.

Hope is one of those fundamentals that is absolutely integral to our human existence, yet it is completely intangible and totally subjective. Without hope in some form, even a minute amount, there is a sense of worthlessness of existence, as though there is no point in continuing.

You sometimes hear people speak of false hope. Personally, I reject the concept that false hope exists. The term 'false hope' is solely based on the judgement of those who are external to the experience of the individual who is living with the hope. In other words, I don't believe in false hope because the individual with the hope still has hope. They may have some doubts around the hope and their hope may be the tiniest glimmer, yet hope still exists as a truth for that individual in their world.

False hope says that the belief and hope that someone has is not worthy of their time and energy. False hope disallows the individual the sovereign right of the truth of their individual experience. False hope seeks to condemn the individual for having any hope in the first place. False hope is disempowering and, I believe, disrespectful. It seems to me to contain an arrogance which says, "I know better than you and you are wrong".

Consider, then, hope in the palliative context. If we think back to the original scenario of hoping for a cure or recovery, then we face a challenge when that possibility is removed by the diagnosis of terminal or life-limiting illness. If there is no hope for a cure or recovery, then how can there be hope? What form can hope take?

Hope in this context takes on a different appearance; it evolves to suit the scenario and the individual. Hope may now look something like this:

- Hope to live long enough to be present for a special event (e.g., wedding, birth, anniversary, birthday)
- Hope to have symptoms well-managed with minimal discomfort
- Hope to tick off some bucket list items
- Hope to see some special people before it's too late
- Hope to leave a legacy of some sort
- Hope to create a good dying and death experience, as defined by the individual
- Hope to not leave a mess behind for loved ones to resolve
- Hope to resolve any unfinished business
- Hope to enjoy simple pleasures
- Hope to experience our faith and belief about what comes after our physical death from a religious or spiritual perspective
- Hope that an alternative course of treatment will provide some benefit
- Hope to know peace, happiness, joy and laughter in the time remaining
- Hope to organise all legal concerns in a timely manner

The list continues on and on.

Hope loses none of its power and can, in fact, provide the catalyst for achieving something specific. I think in this case of my own Mum. As I've mentioned, when she received her terminal diagnosis, her first great-grandchild was already on his way and was due in three months. Her hope was to see that child born before she died, so she did all that she needed to ensure that happened. She had chemotherapy when she had previously said that she never would. She had a great determination in her to hold this babe, and she did. This precious little boy had to do his part in the process by coming four weeks prematurely. Mum got to hold him within a few days of his birth, and less than two weeks later she was gone. I have absolutely no doubt that her hope to see the babe safely delivered into our world was one of the drivers for her experience as she deteriorated so very quickly after she had held him.

Hope is a powerful force in the dying and we need to allow them to define it in ways that are meaningful for them and their journey. It is not for us who are spectating on the sidelines to decide what does and doesn't have significance for someone else's dying and death journey.

Hope is personal, hope is intimate and the responsibility for the definition of hope is solely the domain of each individual sovereign being.

Chapter 19. What Is Keeping Them from Dying?

This is such a tough one, particularly for you as a caring loved one looking on. And that's the crux of the challenge. We have beliefs around timing and what should and should not happen.

We need to remember that we are each on an individual journey that just happens to be shared with others. Our journeys do intertwine and are impacted by each other, but in essence we are all on our own journeys. And each person's journey is determined by them, whether that be on a conscious or sub-conscious level.

I do believe in the concept of soul contracts and that there are energetic experiences and life lessons that we have sought to understand and agreed to undertake. I don't necessarily believe that the detail of how that experience will unfold is part of that soul contract. For example, a person might seek to know the experience of rejection, but the actual manifestation of how the experience will unfold is not detailed in the soul contract.

Now because we do not have conscious recollection of these soul contracts, how can we possibly know what is going on for us, let alone others? So as we look on with love, we may wonder why this loved one is still in our physical reality from our very limited human perspective.

There could be a number of things going on for them:

- They may be waiting to connect or communicate with someone
- There may be a loved one who is resistant to releasing the person on their end journey
- There may be something that they believe they still need to complete or resolve
- There may be some divine timing involved
- There may be other things that have to happen first

The list can go on and on in terms of what may be going on for this person. The main thing is that it is not for us to determine what the right time is for anyone else. We are self-determining individuals, and I believe that choosing our own time of death is one of our sovereign rights. I am very actively involved with Dying with Dignity Queensland, and one of our core requirements for legislation is that a person's wish to end their life must have been clearly and unequivocally expressed by that person themself.

If you have access to and it is appropriate for the beliefs of the person on their end journey, perhaps you might connect with a death doula, death midwife or shamanic practitioner, including yours truly. Someone like this may be able to connect on an energetic level to determine if there is anything that can or needs to be done to assist, but again, it is still up to the person dying to allow that connection and agree to connect in that way.

Other than that, for you as a caring loved ones, it's all about holding this person in pure and unconditional love. It's about creating a peace-filled, sacred environment around them. It's about trusting that there is purpose in their continued physical presence here and accepting that that purpose may never be known. At the end, it's simply about allowing.

Chapter 20. The Road Ahead – Top Tips for Experiencing Grief

At some point in our lives, we will all have to face the loss of someone precious – whether it be a person or 'fur kid'. Yet we receive no guidance or training on how to handle these situations. And our culture isn't exactly open about discussing death.

So where do you turn? How do you get support? What do you do when your world has completely changed? What about that gaping void? How do you honour your loved one? What do you do? What do you not do?

This chapter will give you some tips for navigating your journey in a way that will hopefully make it a bit easier.

My top five tips for experiencing grief are:

- Self-nurturing – if not now, then when?
- Allowing grief to show up however it wants – aka, resistance is futile
- Focussing on the sacred – honour your loved one in ways that are right for you
- Make no apologies, but take no prisoners
- Asking for help if you need it – you don't have to go it alone

Self-nurturing

Yes, it's here again!

This is a time when you need to focus on self-nurturing, self-love and doing what you need to do for you. You are allowed to grieve in a way that works for you, within the bounds of individual responsibility. If you don't allow yourself to nurture yourself at a time when you are emotionally raw and truly in need of it, then when will you?

When my Mum died, I lived in Queensland and Mum lived in Victoria. As you know, I spent the last few weeks of Mum's life with her – caring for her at home for a few days and then overseeing her move to a hospice for the final week and a bit. With my Mum's death, I became the eldest female on that branch of the family's bloodline. I was in my mid-40s.

I have other family, but the major preparation work for Mum's memorial service was my responsibility. I had already promised Mum that I would do the eulogy. So I had the eulogy to write, the slide presentation to prepare, the music to go with that, the orders of service to design and get printed. All this when my Mum had just died.

While all this was happening, I also had to organise the clearing of Mum's unit as it had been rented. My hubby and teenage daughter and I were all staying in Mum's small one-bedroom unit – so it was cramped. remember, my Mum had just died.

On the day of the service, I got there early, making sure that everything was in order. I gave the eulogy and after the service played hostess to all of the people in attendance – around 100. I moved around the room, making sure that everyone was okay, checking on Mum's friends and consoling and comforting them. Remember, my Mum had died.

Once the service was over, I had two more days before my hubby and daughter flew home. I was flying home three days after my hubby and daughter left – less than two weeks after Mum had died. There were things listed online for sale; there was stuff going to op shops left, right and centre; there was stuff to send home with my hubby and daughter; I also had to work out what I would be able to take home. There was co-ordination with friends who were helping move the bigger items, and of course there was the cleaning of Mum's unit to be done. Again, all of this when my Mum had just died.

Where on earth was the self-nurturing in that? There was none. I was on autopilot and it was only on reflection that I saw how I was trying to be all things to everyone, comforting everyone else and consoling them, particularly at the service, when it was *my* Mum who had died!

I don't share it in this way to sound like a martyr, because that's not what it was about. But so often we focus on the things we believe are important at the time, without allowing time for ourselves during the process.

When I got home, naturally I fell in a heap . . . actually, it really started just before the final load left Mum's unit as I was finishing the cleaning. I had lost my very precious Mum and yet I had not allowed myself any time to grieve.

Thankfully, I was able to do that when I got home. I slept lots, I went to the beach, and I did not rush back into working – even though being self-employed meant no money coming in. I knew that I had to allow myself that time or that it would come back and bite me on the butt. This was a profoundly powerful insight. And it makes for a great lead into my next tip.

Allowing grief to show up however it wants

When it comes to grief, there are no absolutes save one. You will have fabulous days, you will have not-so-fabulous days and you will have days where you just want to curl up in the foetal position and cry like there's no tomorrow. And you can go from having a fabulous day to the foetal position in a matter of seconds. You might even get to string together a number of fabulous days and think that you are returning to some sort of normality and then something will trigger a memory – be it a sight, a sound, a smell, some music or any other reminder – and you will instantly feel like a rug has been pulled out from underneath you and you start to wonder if you will ever feel "normal" again – whatever that is. That's how grief works.

When grief appears, the very best thing you can do is just to allow it to be. If you need to cry – do it. If you need to sleep – do it. If you want to bake up a storm – do it. If you need some time alone – do it. One thing I have learned from personal experience is that if you think that you can tie it all up in a neat little package and say "That's it, all done and dusted", then consider yourself warned. Your grief will come back and bite you on the butt stronger and harder than you ever imagined . . . and generally at the worst possible time.

Why is that? Grief, like any other strong emotion, occurs for a reason. You only feel deep grief if you have felt deep love.

If you suppress anger, hatred, pain or frustration, you will plateau for a while, but over time it will build up inside you like a pressure cooker and one day explode. Equally, if you don't allow yourself to fully experience the pleasant emotions – excitement, joy, happiness, bliss, passion – that, too, will cause you to plateau for a while. However instead of exploding you will eventually cease being able to connect with those feelings – or any others. Again, look at Brené Brown's work. She expressed it best in her talk on vulnerability when she said that we aren't able to selectively numb what we feel.

There is nothing brave or courageous about 'soldiering on', which is a very different energy to consciously choosing to do something as a distraction. By all means, seek to change your mood or make yourself feel a bit better by doing something that you enjoy – that's actually empowering yourself. However, you will not do anyone any favours, especially yourself, by 'pushing through the pain'.

The death of your loved one, be it fur kid or human, has left a gaping hole in your life. And it's one that will never be filled, because nothing and no one can ever take the place of what you shared with them. In time, hopefully you will learn to live with the hole, to find new ways of being and of living without their presence. Grieve for their physical absence in your life; grieve for what may have been the promise of tomorrow, but now is not; grieve for the times shared that cannot be shared again.

Allow yourself to fully acknowledge that your life has changed and realise that will take some adjusting.

Allow yourself to be with the rawness, particularly in the first weeks and even first few months. I find that the big occasions I am mostly prepared for, but it's the unexpected triggers that bring me undone. For instance, my sister died in 2008, and there are still some little things that set me off. There are no time limits on grief and there are certainly no 'shoulds'. Grief is the epitome of a unique journey.

Within the bounds of individual responsibility, allow your grief to be.

Where exactly are those bounds, and how, amidst your grief, can you tell where they are? This is one that you need to answer within the context of how you live your life. I would suggest holding the concept of ensuring that everything you do and don't do is with the intention of being for the highest and best good of all concerned.

Focussing on the sacred

Your relationship with your loved one was unique – just as was everyone else's. Doing something that was special for the two of you could be something that might horrify someone else in their life. My sister Bess was big into glitter. She wasn't a girly-girl, but she totally loved bling and glitter. She worked for a funeral company and her best friend still does. This beautiful friend and a couple of others were charged with preparing Bess for the viewing.

We'd had viewings for both my Gran and Dad and they just hadn't looked as I'd known them to look, so I wasn't planning on another viewing. But something said to me that Bess's would be different, and it was. I think maybe because the people preparing her had known Bess so well in real life, they knew what she was meant to look like. The make-up was perfect and she truly looked like she was just sleeping. But the best bit was that they had surrounded her in the coffin with a truckload of glitter – in all different colours and sizes.

When we scattered her ashes, some extra glitter was added in then as well. This was all totally perfect for who she was, but I dare say that some other people might not have approved.

There is a great movie called *The Last of the Blonde Bombshells* starring Dame Judi Dench as the character Elizabeth. If you love World War II-era music, I highly recommend it. The story line goes that after Elizabeth's husband dies, she begins reminiscing about when she played sax in a band during the war and starts a quest to get the band back together, almost half a century later. Elizabeth is very close with her 12-year-old granddaughter Joanna and asks her for some advice. The script goes something like this . . .

Elizabeth: Joanna, I need your advice.

Joanna: I'll try.

Elizabeth: What's the best way of showing respect for the dead?

Joanna: That's easy. You go on living.

And that's about the size of it. While there might be times we wish we were the ones who were dead, we are not. We are still living. It may sound like a cliché, but you truly can use the death of someone special to you as a catalyst for changing your own life.

It doesn't even have to be someone you know. I was deeply moved after both 9/11 and the Boxing Day tsunami to a realization about just how frail life can be and how most of us do not have conscious awareness of when our time will be up. I know of someone who experienced the Boxing Day tsunami first hand, and they certainly live their life to the fullest now.

Honour your loved one in a way that is authentic to both you and them. We have a sort of shrine at home containing pictures of those we have loved and lost, along with some other special treasures. My Mum, for example, used to make the absolute best shortbreads, and she would make tens of dozens of them and give them as gifts at Christmas. I made some the first Christmas after Mum died as it just didn't feel right without them.

My Dad had booked a flight to Antarctica which he didn't get to take before he died. My sister did the flight and took his ashes with her. Another family member did a cruise to Antarctica a little while after my sister died – they took some of her ashes with them. Some people might find that all a bit weird, but for them it was completing a circle.

I've seen stories on Facebook – one was of a family who made a sandpit on top of their little boy's grave so that his brother could play with him. Another was of a person who left a bucket of tennis balls at a park with a note for anyone to play with them with their dogs, as that's what their dog had loved to do.

Whatever it is that feels right for you (again, within the bounds of individual responsibility), just do it! It will help massively with the grieving process and with your learning how to live without that precious someone in your life.

Make no apologies, but take no prisoners

This might sound a bit weird, but it follows on from allowing for your grief and honouring your loved one in an authentic way. There's a word that I ban when I am doing my spiritual counselling work with my clients, and that is 'sorry'. You have absolutely nothing to apologise for when it comes to feeling and expressing your grief. So many times I see and hear people apologise for crying or for grieving. So many clients feel that they can't talk to anyone about what they are feeling because it will make the other person uncomfortable.

Right here, right now, I say to you, "Who gives a stuff?" You have had someone precious in your world die, so you are actually allowed to grieve – strange as it may seem. And if someone else becomes uncomfortable because of your grief, it is more about them and what may or may not be going for them rather than you.

But you also need to allow others to grieve in ways that are right for them. When my Dad died, we had a family lunch at a local pub after the service. A family member disappeared for hours and did not join us for lunch. At the time, I remember feeling hurt and angry.

Now, with the benefit of hindsight and a bit of maturity, I can acknowledge that this person was doing what was right for them. They needed some space to just be with what they were feeling, and right at that moment, they needed to be on their own. I was hurt and disappointed, and that was part of my own authentic response. But I also had to allow this other person to be in the space they needed.

We don't have the right to expect someone to grieve in the same way that we do. Just because someone is not crying their heart out, for instance, does not mean that they are feeling any less pain than you are.

Allow your grief to be in ways that are authentic for you, but also allow others the same right.

Asking for help if you need it

Yep, it's this one again. You will know within yourself if your grief is overwhelming you to the degree where you need some assistance. If you are feeling this, seek some help. Please. There are numerous ways that you can get assistance. There are phone services like Lifeline, and if your loved one died as a result of cancer, all of the state cancer organisations have phone services that can assist. Psychologists and other types of professional counsellors can help you. If you belong to a religious organisation, it will generally be able to provide assistance as well.

Chapter 21. A Special Ceremony

The last thing I wish to leave with you is a special little ceremony that I was gifted while doing some shamanic journey work. It's not long, and it is a ceremony that I undertake when a client has left our physical realm.

I don't know if you know this, but a flame casts no shadow. Hold a lit match against a wall, then throw another light source on the match. You will see no shadow from the flame. You need this knowledge for the ceremony.

Centre yourself, take a deep breath and light a candle while saying the following words:

We light this candle to symbolise the transition from a being of love and light that casts a shadow to a being of love and light that does not.

And so it is.

www.ingramcontent.com/pod-product-compliance
Ingram Content Group UK Ltd.
Pitfield, Milton Keynes, MK11 3LW, UK
UKHW041828200726
13854UKWH00002BA/886

9 780987 419842